Faithfully Fearless

Kristen Sandmire

Kristen Sandmire

Jeremiah 29:11

Contents

1

Rooted In Love

I've gotten to a point in my life that not much intimidates me anymore because I've learned how amazing the power of God is. However, writing this book and the whole idea of realizing how much information I would need to reference in order to actually make this dream come true, did make me feel slightly intimidated. I have learned though that if I just take the first step, God will give me what I need in order to accomplish what He has laid on my heart for me to do.

I'm just a small town girl born and raised in the little town of Clarksville, Tennessee. Though I've never really ventured out and seen much else of this world other than the beach a few times and a trip to Denver, Colorado for work, I've still seen a lot. I've never had the desire to leave this little town that has actually grown tremendously since I was child, well mainly because everything I needed was right here. Other than my dad and little brother living in a different state for a very short time period, my mom, all of my grandparents, my aunts, uncles, and cousins all live here right here in Clarksville. Now you see why I had no reason to leave, right?

I don't think anyone's childhood could top mine. I'm pretty humble and avoid bragging about anything but I will brag all day long about my childhood. It was absolutely amazing and something I wish every child got to experience. My mom and dad divorced when I was two and they both remarried, so I went from having two sets of grandparents to having four sets. You don't know good times until you've celebrated a holiday from sun up until sun down. It always blew my mind how Santa showed up to all those homes to leave gifts for me. He was really on top of his game back then. One cool thing is that my birthday is on Christmas. Well, it's cool to most people because they think I get double the gifts, but for gifting purposes I kind of got shorted. Not from my parents of course but it was an easy thing to forget on such a special holiday. I mean Christmas is all about Jesus anyway and honestly I'm just honored to share a birthday with Him. That's the coolest part about it for me.

I grew up living with my mom but I would go visit my dad and stay with him every other weekend. He would come and pick me up on Friday night and we would spend the weekend making memories. On Saturdays we could be found somewhere on my dad's parents' beautiful piece of two acre property. They had two huge gardens there that combined had to be at least a full acre of food. I could be found playing baseball with my grandmother who was always so active with us grandchildren, sitting out on the swing with my dad underneath this huge tree that they eventually had cut down, or pushing baby dolls in a carriage up and down the hallways of this beautiful country home that my grandfather built with his own two hands. Sundays were for church and a quick stop at the little country convenient store down the road that sold barbecue. You can't beat a day full of Jesus and barbecue sandwiches; at least you couldn't when it came to my childhood.

My dad's side of the family is huge! My dad has three siblings and each sibling has two children, including my dad. At any family gathering we would all pile up in my grandmother's dining room and eat the absolute best cooking I've ever tasted in my life. There is something about country living that is just so special. Even more special is country cooking. I grew up on the best food known to man! Because of such a large family, we wouldn't all fit at the dining room table so they would pull out the kids table. It wasn't unusual for all of us cousins to argue our way into sitting next to our favorite cousin if an argument was required. The dining room was pretty big but it still required us to squeeze in there. All eighteen of us would hold hands as a family member led us in prayer. When faith is rooted in a childhood, it's really hard to ever uproot it.

Some of my most memorable memories as a child came from that two acre piece of property. Staying out there was always such an adventure on the weekends. Before papa Ray passed away, he and granny Mabel would spend a lot of their time at the campground fishing and enjoying their time together, just the two of them. They kept the camper right behind their house when they weren't at the campground and for some odd reason; I was drawn to that camper. Every time I went out there I would want to go in this camper that always felt well over one hundred degrees and pretend it was home. It was like my imagination grew as soon as I hit that property.

Granny had everything I needed out there to be a teacher, a mom, an artist, a base ball player a professional tricycle rider. I mean the possibilities were endless out there. The best part about all of these endless options was that granny would get just as involved in them as I did and it doesn't get more special than that from a child's perspective. She would build us tents with all of the dining room table chairs and would proceed to crawl right into the fort with us. My favorite moments for tent building were when a storm was coming. We'd get this big ole tent built and it would be nearly dark in the middle of the day because of the storm brewing and we would camp out until it was over. It never occurred to me that if it was a real serious storm our fort wouldn't keep me protected but that's the beauty of a child's innocence I suppose.

Papa Ray passed away when I was six years old from lung cancer. I don't remember a whole lot about him but I know that he was a hard working man that smoked tobacco out of one of those cool looking pipes. I can still remember what that smelled like, even twenty-five years later. They tell me that I used to crawl up in his lap and we would both have a spoon along with a gallon bucket of Neapolitan ice cream that we would eat together. My mom told me that he taught me to tie my shoes. From all of the stories about him that I've heard, they picked the most patient man to teach a toddler to tie her shoes, that's for sure.

I have heard all about him growing up and I can't figure out if some of the memories I think I have from him are true memories or are from stories I've heard or pictures I've seen. Either way, I know he was a gentle man. He was quiet and if he had a temper it was something I never witnessed. He was a genuine and laid back individual which is no doubt what helped contribute to the best love story I've ever seen. Papa Ray and Granny Mabel were the epitome of what a real love store looks like. There was truly nothing sweeter. God was at the center of their love story and it was something that was very apparent if you witnessed it. If I could imagine where their love stood with each other on the day my Papa Ray passed away, I'd picture it stood on the same feelings that it stood on when they ran away to get married after only three months of dating, but 48 years stronger.

After he passed away, family events changed a little bit. They weren't as often and even during the holidays, it wasn't as packed in the dining room as it used to be. I never really thought to ask why either but I'll just assume that like everything else in life that changes, so did our routine as a family. That's the beautiful thing about memories though, they last forever and the thought of a memory brings back all of the same feelings that existed while making the memory. That's why we are encouraged to live in the moment.

If someone's faith could be a trophy recipient, my granny Mabel's would have won first place. A walk through her home would have revealed it just in pictures and items that hung on her walls. She loved the Lord more than anything in life and was by far the most Christian woman I've ever known. Her faith was unforgettable and I can still hear her singing hymns through the hallways of her Jesus filled home.

Even with eight grandchildren, she had enough love to share with every single one of us, and it was always shared fair, evenly distributed. I don't think she had a favorite or cared for one more than the other. It never seemed that way. Pure and genuine love poured out of her to everyone, not just her family. When I think of how she loved every individual she knew, I think of Jesus.

My mom's side of the family was small in comparison to my dad's. My grandfather was military so my childhood memories with him are few and far between. My grandmother was the cafeteria manager at a middle school so her work hours were flexible enough to fit me right in, especially on the days when my mom would work late. Meme would pick me up from daycare and take me by my mom's work to see her and to pick out a book. Mom worked retail basically right across the street from my daycare center so it was convenient for us to stop by there on the way to Meme's house. That was always our first stop. Our second stop was McDonalds drive-thru where she would order me a hamburger and fries. I still remember sitting in the back seat of her car and barely being able to see over the window pane down to the flower bed in McDonalds drive thru where there were little wood stakes pushed into the ground on which all of the McDonald's characters sat on top of.

Meme spoiled me rotten. My mom has two brothers and neither of them had children so the likelihood of me being spoiled was pretty high and I am unashamed to say I was. That woman found any excuse to do anything for me. I'm sure her explanation to my grandfather was always entertaining to hear. He was military and very frugal so you better have had a good excuse to spend money when you presented him with a recent purchase you had made.

Holidays were just as special at Meme and Papa's as they were at Granny and Papa Ray's house, but not as big. I guess you can say I experienced both ends of the spectrum when it came to family. I got a little dose of both. They both were special in their own ways that's for sure. The most common denominator between the two of them was family time and to me, that's what was most important.

Meme passed away when I was nine years old from lung cancer. I have some pretty fond memories of some of the special things we did together and that she did for me. She always had what seemed like an endless amount of chocolate milk stored in her refrigerator. She would deliver it to me while I watched one of my favorite movies on the couch, in a yellow sippy cup with a white top and a picture of Speedy Gonzales from the cartoon on the side of it. Which now that I think about it, I was never interested in that show so that cup must have been passed down to me from my mom's younger brother Michael who was only fifteen years older than me.

I was truly blessed with some amazing people in my life that I am so thankful to call my family. You seriously can't beat a childhood as awesome as mine was. You don't realize how much you reference your child hood as you get older, but I'm telling you, I reference it constantly. It is the foundation of which my entire life was built on and let me tell you, it was solid. If you can bless a child with an unforgettable childhood, you've accomplished something that money can't buy and an adult can't be taught. These little things in life are priceless.

2

He Comforts Us

Mom remarried after her and my dad divorced. She married a man who had two children of his own. At this point in my life, Kristen Jo would become my primary point of contact. My step-dad had a child with same name as me and the only way to keep it from being too confusing was using our middle names in addition to our first. We got a few odd looks from those who didn't know we were step sisters. I had a step-brother as well and he was almost a year older than me. Mt step-sister and I were six months to the day apart. I can still hear mom saying it just like that when someone asked if me and Kristen were twins. At that point in my life I really didn't understand the concept of sharing I suppose. It had always been just me up until that point so the sharing department wasn't my area to take pride in. I was a spoiled child who had been all alone on my mom's side of the family so this new role as being the middle child was tough to understand being the spoiled princess I was.

My step-dad was a huge part of my life for twelve years. We had been a family of five for so long, I finally just took the step out of everything and they became, dad, sister, and brother. No steps required there. We lived like any other typical five member family does from the ages of four to twelve. Most week nights were spent at the ball field for softball and baseball or in the gym for gymnastics for me and my sister. Mom worked retail and my step-dad was a mechanic so their schedules would change from time to time. They split most of the chores; rather it was picking us up from daycare or giving all three of us a bath. One chore they didn't split was the cooking. My mom had a one hit wonder and that was lasagna. My step-dad though, that man could throw down in the kitchen, still does. The main thing I remember about the two of them from my childhood is that they always made sure we were taken care of. The three of us kids never did without.

My memory gets a little patchy when I reflect on that time in my life because it feels like everything happened so quickly. My Meme got really sick in 1996 and was diagnosed with cancer. My mom became her primary care giver and was at her side through it all until the day she passed away. My step dad was the glue that held our family together during all of this. I can only imagine the pressure mom was under and all of the emotions she experienced not only witnessing her mom being so sick, but also watching her basically die. Not to mention all she felt like she was neglecting at her home where her family was. I can't imagine my step-dad's pressure either. He went from having a team player parent to three kids, to taking on all of the efforts it took to basically be a single parent. Mom did the best she could through this time in our lives but she was mainly taking care of her mom. They both held down a full time job through all of this too which was crazy. This segment of our lives was life changing to say the least. It's amazing how much you appreciate when you grow up to be an adult and look back on your childhood.

My mom and my Meme shared a very close bond. When Meme passed away in January of 1997 it rocked our entire family's world. In August, Meme's dad would also pass away that year and mom would be the executor of his estate. The next two years were really a blur. I know my step-dad, step-sister, and step-brother were still there on New Years Eve of the year 2000 because I remember sitting suspenseful on my step-dad's lap during Y2K in my Y2K shirt waiting for the clock to turn over to midnight. It had to have been within the next year that everything changed. At numerous failed attempts to make things work out, my step-dad and my mom would split up and back to being an only child I went. This time, twelve years later, being a single child wasn't as exciting. I missed my normal.

As an adult, I think back on that event for all of our lives and wonder how it affected them. There was no doubt that my step-dad loved me as if I was his and mom loved my step-sister and step-brother as if they were hers. For mom, bless her heart, I'm sure she blamed herself but if she ever did, she never voiced it to me. I can't imagine how my step-dad felt during all of that chaos either.

I've learned something about death and that is that it requires a process called the grieving process. Grieving is something that everyone does differently. There is no right way and there is no wrong way to grieve. I've also learned to be humble when it comes to witnessing someone else who may be grieving differently than I would because we truly never know what's next in our own lives so to judge someone else for the way they handle something is just not right.

Shortly after the tragic year of 1997, my mom picked up something that she used to help her grieve, addiction. My mom and step-dad sheltered us kids from knowing the full extent of everything that was happening, but I can only imagine that this new lifestyle for my mom was a big contribution to their divorce. Mom and I would start new on our own but we would live quite a bit different than we did twelve years prior.

During my elementary school years, mom didn't miss anything. She was sure to sign up for every field trip and wouldn't miss the opportunity to come have lunch with me at school. All of the other kids at school loved her so much and she treated them no different than she treated me. She is one of those moms that go above and beyond for her child. She is that mom that no matter how old you get and no matter what happens in life, you never forget that potential she had and the effort she put into everything. Love is shown through actions and it surely showed up in my mom. That's the memory of my mom I clung to through the most chaotic moments that addiction brought.

I can't say enough about middle school. My experience in middle school was quite a bit different than most children's I'm sure. Mom's addiction had finally surfaced and could no longer be hidden. As soon as it was a known issue for her, it was time to at least attempt to get her help. I stayed with her best friend for a few weeks during my seventh grade year while mom went to rehab. After her third rehab center, she finally seemed like she was starting to really get better and was actually trying. I remember going to visit her at the last rehab facility she had been checked into. She gave me so much hope for our future while I was there. We were in this big conference room with this big dry erase board. I don't know why but I remember being so scared and intimated by this place. Even at this point, I didn't realize the true seriousness of what was going on or to what extent she was actually struggling with addiction. Unfortunately for some, rehab just doesn't heal what is truly broken. Luckily when this addiction stepped up and made an appearance into my mom's life, so did my uncle Michael.

Michael was such a blessing to me during this time in my life. He was a constant and he had moved in with us shortly after mom and my step-dad got a divorce. He was there for all of the new scenes I would encounter with mom. If she had taken too much medication she was known for falling asleep with a cigarette, dozing off sitting up and even sometimes completely unresponsive. Michael was so helpful for me through this new beginning and new way of life. He would find opportunities to take me with him to his friends' house. He would take me out to diners for a late night; spur of the moment dinner or even sometimes for ice cream. Michael and I became really close during this chapter of my life. I think he saw me as a little sister and I saw him like an older brother and even a dad for some moments. He was the coolest dude I knew. It was during that time period that every new teenager goes through and experiences. That period that we are trying to figure out exactly who we are and when we want to be just like that older group of cool kids. Michael was that cool kid and I wanted to be like him and all of his friends when I grew up.

Michael was pretty protective so when I met this super cute guy in high school, he definitely wasn't as sure about this new relationship I was attempting to establish as I was. The guy had just gotten out of a little bit of trouble, so looking back I can understand Michael's concern, but at that age, there's something about a troubled guy that just catches a girl's attention. He was eighteen and still lived at home with his mom and dad. I had to be careful about anything serious when it came to relationships back then because mom's lifestyle was one that I felt like would make any guy turn me down. We were like a package deal and if someone wouldn't accept her then I couldn't even give it an opportunity. She was my main priority.

It couldn't have been as easy as he's made it look, falling in love with a girl who was basically attached to her mom at the hip. My life literally revolved around her. He accepted it though and it didn't take long for him to understand why I loved her so much and why it was so hard to just walk away from all of the chaos. At the center of that dark addiction, was a beautiful heart that radiated its love to everyone it met.

My mom was my best friend. Our bond was something that I wish every mother and daughter got to experience. It was so special to both of us. I was her only child so that alone gave her the ability to love me with her whole heart. Being a mom wasn't the only thing she was amazing at. Her personality was one that if you'd come in contact with, you'd never forget it. She cared about every soul she met and if your path crossed over hers, there was no doubt she saw you as her own family member. I've never seen so much love and compassion in one person and honestly I don't know how it all fit in there but it did, and I'm just thankful God blessed me with such a remarkable mother.

That troubled guy hung around for a lot longer than I ever expected him to. He was there every step of the way. He played hard to get there in the beginning but that's typical for high school I suppose. For three years we would break up on and off but never more than two weeks at a time. It was hard to stay away from each other because of all of the mutual friends we had. There would be parties hosted and I would go with my girlfriends and he would be there with his guy friends. It was kind of sweet looking back on.

By the time I had turned eighteen and graduated high school in the spring of 2006, three years after that troubled guy named Ryan had walked into my life, he had accomplished quite a bit and troubled was now definitely a part of his past. Was this real? Had I met my soul mate at the age of fifteen? Someone pinch me. I think I'll keep him forever.

3

Trust In Him

After a long battle with dementia that turned into Alzheimer's, my precious, Jesus filled hearted, Granny Mabel passed away in March of 2006. That is a heart wrenching illness to witness. She ended up getting pneumonia shortly before she passed away and I will never forget the doctor saying that he couldn't hear her heart beat because pneumonia had filled up her lungs so much. She was finally with Papa Ray, the only love she ever knew in her life.

Now that I was eighteen, mom said it would be okay for Ryan to move in with us to help with bills. Plus with three years under our belt as an item, it seemed okay. Mom was in the process of getting disability/social security so the money I made at jobs I would go to right after I got out of high-school every day, was our only source of income. I started working at a pizza joint when I was fifteen and have had a job ever since. If there is one thing to teach your kids that will stick with them for life, teach them the value of money.

Mom dated a guy named Patrick who would help us when he could. They started dating when I was fourteen and he would always help us out if we came up short rather it was with bills or groceries. Patrick came to stay with us every now and then but he cared for both of his parents, so he was needed there most nights. With Ryan moving in it would help tremendously. We had a finished basement at my mom's so that would be perfect for him to set up his little bachelor pad.

Right before Ryan moved in, our family was struck with tragedy. My mom and I went out school shopping for my first semester of college. As you can imagine, I housed so much excitement about this. My mom had been approved for disability so this was the first opportunity she had to take me school shopping since before high school. She was completely sober all day (which was huge for her because of her anxiety struggle with being out in public) and we had just wrapped up one of the best days we had spent together in a long time. We had just left the mall and were headed home when she got a phone call. On the other end of the phone was one of Michael's best friends and all she said was that something serious was going on and we needed to get to his apartment. Michael was a handy man so he fit the job perfectly of being the maintenance man at the apartment complex that he lived in. I remember mom making me pull the car over into a veterinarian parking lot while she was on the phone until she was able to gather the information she was receiving. When she hung up, she simply said, "Drive to Michael's house." There was no way that she could hide that something serious was wrong. When you're genuine, you just can't hide emotion.

When I mentioned earlier that Clarksville has grown since I was little, it has. In this town there's a hill known as, "Boot Hill" that's basically the main connection between downtown Clarksville and Ft. Campbell military base. As you can imagine, it stays pretty busy. On a normal afternoon it can take anywhere from five to ten minutes to get through that congested area. We had to travel this hill in order to get to Michael's apartment that day and it was right around the time the hill gets backed up. The five to ten minutes we sat there felt like forty-five minutes. Having my flashers on did us no good at all in bumper to bumper traffic. Didn't anyone else realize that we have an emergency and we need them all to move so we can get to Michael?

As soon as I got through that traffic I gunned it. I have a lead foot just like my mom. My dad has even mentioned that before. I guess he had his fair share of excitement and panic riding passenger in her car. Mom always sped up to a turn she was about to make and then slammed the brakes to make the turn. I did not inherit that particular driving skill from her, thank goodness. Speeding on the other hand, yes, I did inherit that. Mom's driving would always send me into a come to Jesus moment. Praying endlessly kept me in constant communication with the Lord while riding in the car with her. It really wasn't that bad but this day, her inherited lead foot I had adopted, came in handy.

Michael lived right off of a main road here in town and you could see the back of his apartment form the main road if there weren't any leaves on the trees. It was the end of August though so I couldn't see a thing from the main road. As we made that turn onto his road, it was obvious there was something major wrong. There were at least six cop cars, a few unmarked cars, and a van ambulance. I don't' think I had ever seen a van ambulance before this day and I know I will never see them the same. Surrounding Michael's apartment complex and his truck was yellow crime scene tape. I learned the harsh treatment a car could truly take that day. I did not even allow the car to stop moving before I threw it into park. Mom and I jumped out in tears and ran to the scene together. There were police officers walking in and out. They were doing everything from collecting any finger prints on the door knobs to trying to keep us updated and informed of what was going on and what they found when they got there.

Right before they wrapped up from investigating the scene, they asked us to go inside one of the ladies apartments that were across the street from his so that they could remove his body from the scene. They brought his body out and put it into that ambulance van. That feeling I had when I came from the woman's apartment and reality hit that his deceased body was in the back of the van was unexplainable. I will always relate death to an ambulance in the form of a van.

The days to come were awful. One moment that even twelve years later stands very vivid in my memory was my grandfather's reaction when we told him. There's one thing about a seventy-eight year old retired paratrooper that served in the military nearly thirty years and served in Vietnam and that is that they don't cry, but this day, one did. I can't imagine his heartache that day but I can assure you that I only got a small glimpse of it. Having to bury a child has to be the absolute worst thing in life that one can ever experience.

In an attempt to share with everyone who attended the funeral service, the special and irreplaceable bond that Michael and I shared, I wrote a eulogy. My only goal at this point was to get up and have the strength to read it in front of all of these people. Public speaking was not my thing back then and that has not changed a bit but I knew I could do it for him. Through some occasional tears and a countless amount of deep breaths, I did it.

As you can imagine, this hit my mom hard. Because of her habit of dealing with the tough things in life, I knew this meant I needed to be on high alert for her addiction purposes. She had gotten to a point that in an attempt to numb all of the feelings she would experience, she would over take her medicine. I always tried to stay one step ahead of her when it came to her pill addiction but she had gotten pretty sneaky by this point. By this point in my life and my journey and experiences with her pill addiction I was very cautious with certain things. If I called her phone and she didn't answer the phone I wouldn't go home by myself. Luckily this night, I had two really good friends with me.

Three nights after we buried Michael, I walked in our front door and all I could see from the front door were her feet. She was laying face down in the kitchen floor, thank God still breathing. Two friends of mine and Ryan picked her up off of the floor for me and took her to her bed where she slept the remainder of the night. It wasn't uncommon for me to go back and check on her periodically through the night to make sure she was still breathing. These types of episodes would always prompt a thorough clean out of bags and drawers because those are the places she was known to hide her pill stash the most.

There was no real method to the amount of days she would stay under the influence or how much time passed before her next episode occurred so it was usually a surprise. I could leave for work in the morning and she would be fine and I could call at lunch and I could tell in the manner that she was talking that we were knocking on the door way of another binge. Typically she would go no longer than a month without a binge, even if it was only two days.

As I stated earlier, I am my mom's only child. This wasn't something I could take vacations from or take a few days off here and there, this was full time. There was no off switch for this or a pause button. Her addiction controlled my life and controlled the majority of decisions I made. Something as simple as hanging out with my friends was always based off of mom's condition. If I had any doubt in my mind that mom was even the least bit buzzing, I wouldn't leave. Of course this isn't at all how she wanted me to live and she didn't want me to worry about her but that's what was so ironic about this situation because she had always been the type of loving and concerned mom that I was trying to be for her.

Shortly after Michael passed away, Ryan moved in. This gave me some peace because it wasn't just me anymore. The trauma that comes with some of the things I saw made me scared to be alone in the moments that she would be under the influence. Having Ryan there would be comforting and would allow me to sleep a little better at night.

I started a new job about a week after we buried Michael. I was starting at the same retail store that my mom was employed at for eighteen years but she had quit working there a few years before I started. She was a key holder and the Sporting Goods manager for the first ten years she was employed there. She eventually became the human resource manager the last eight she was there and she was the perfect fit for that job. When you are any type of manager in retail, your scheduled time to be off is never a guarantee which explains all of the time I spent with my Meme when I was younger. I of course didn't take on

27

either management position that she was such a pro at when I was employed there, but I did make a good sales associate. I worked in the women's apparel department and could fold a shirt like a champ.

I had just started my first semester of college with a plan to get my bachelor's degree in accounting. College classes made for a tricky work schedule. I felt like I would never get the choice to work days with all of my friends and my boyfriend because I always had to work night shift hours. That's when all of my friends were off though and that wasn't even fair. Some nights I would come home to a handful of Ryan's friends all hanging out in the basement playing video games or making music. They could also be known to be hanging out upstairs with mom.

Mom was more than just a mom to me she was a mom to all of my friends. In her presence was where you could find a lot of mine and Ryan's friends if they were going through a moment in their lives that they needed reliable wisdom for. Her best asset was her ears and an open mind. She would always listen to anything you had going on in your personal life even if her own was in shambles and she would go on to find it within her to conjure up the best advice she could to help get you through your stuff. She had a heart like Jesus.

I mentioned that Ryan made music so yes, of course I will elaborate. Ryan houses a lot of talent within him and if you know him, you know that. At one point in his life, his dream was to become a well known and signed hip-hop music artist. His lyrical talent when it came to this music he wrote was seriously something you would hear on the radio. I was always blown away at how he thought of this word and made this word connect back to the word he mentioned in the previous line and then somehow not only made these words rhyme but they would all be related and the killer part of all of that was that it always made sense. When he moved in with me and mom, he built a studio booth in the garage. It was legit. It had two parts. On one side you would go in and mix and master the music being recorded and on the other side you would go in, put on your set of headphones, and listen to your beat of choice, and bam, record the song you wrote on the one thousand dollar high quality microphone that Ryan invested in. Our house was the place to be during this chapter and I can guarantee you that this is where our entire group of friends could be found most weekends. I can't tell you how many stories I heard through these lyrics each individual wrote from their heart but I can tell you how it changed my perspective of music. It was something I grew to have major respect for and haven't seen the same since.

Over the course of the next few years we would spend our weekends partying and living life to the fullest. I never really partied as much as everyone else during this part of my life because I was always playing the role of mother hen. It was almost like it had been ingrained into my soul to always be on standby. Mom was pretty cool about it all as long as we stayed downstairs if we were going to be loud. By this point I was twenty-one and the majority of my friends were at least twenty-one. There may or may not have been a few under age but that's neither here nor there and what's living without living on the edge anyway right?!

4

Bound In Love

It is crazy how quickly the college years go by even though during that time it doesn't feel like it. Before I knew it, I was walking across another stage but this time it was with a Bachelors Degree in Accounting instead of a High School Diploma. Michael had promised me he would be at this one since he missed my high school graduation. That made it bitter sweet. December 2010, one of my biggest goals in life had been attained. I was so proud of myself for accomplishing this big milestone. It was tough keeping up with my mom, with all of my friends, with work, and with college. Thankfully, I had the wonderful opportunity to spend my last two years of college working as a courier for a law firm. They were so flexible there so with each semester change, I would just change my schedule up and just show up when my classes were over for the day. It was a great experience for me and even though I'm no law expert, I still learned a lot of things working there. I met so many people on my daily post office trips, bank runs, and court house adventures. If I had an apple watch back then, because of all of the walking I did, I'd imagine it would tell me to rest.

Shortly after graduation, wedding planning went into full swing. At this point Ryan and I had just recently celebrated our seven year dating anniversary so it was time to make it official. I had worked hard enough trying to convince him to marry me that we were due to go ahead and go through with it. He had promised me over the past seven years that I was his forever and we could be together until our last breath but marriage wasn't something that he particularly had on his agenda. Thankfully, he finally gave in and it was time to celebrate with a long awaited wedding. As you can imagine, our friends were ecstatic. This was something they dreamed of as much as I did. We always won couple of the year in our group of friends because we are the only relationship that had survived as long as we had. During teenage years and early twenties, that's pretty special I suppose.

During the course of all of the wedding planning, I interviewed for a job working for a boot company in the credit department. In April of 2011, I became the newest credit department employee for the boot company and just like that, a new chapter of life started. All of my jobs in the past required some type of uniform but here I could basically wear anything I wanted to work. I could go to lunch whenever I wanted to and had a choice of what my hours would be. I could come in at seven or eight and as long as I got eight hours of work in that day, they didn't care which one I chose. I chose the seven to four shift because I am a morning person and it made sense to have a longer afternoon when I got off.

At this point, Ryan and I had discussed buying a house and moving out of moms after we tied the knot but nothing was set in stone and honestly this was a touchy subject for me. As much as I wanted to start my own life with Ryan I was really struggling with the idea of, "Letting go" of mom. It was touched on every now and then but I kind of put it in the back of my mind for now because one, we had a wedding to plan and two; it didn't feel serious enough for me to spend a lot of my time thinking about. The few times I had brought it to my mom's attention, she was clearly not a fan of the idea at all. She would even tell me that I needed to get out and start my own life with him but her face told a different story. I felt like I could see her broken heart through her eyes as she told me that Ryan and I needed this.

Back to the main priority at that current moment, wedding planning. It was approaching rather quickly and I couldn't help but think about everything that needed to be done before November. Because I went straight to college from high school, this was the first semester in seventeen years that I wasn't in school and wasn't spending all of my time on school work. What better way to spend it than planning a wedding right?! This was more stressful than school. I had seven bridesmaids so that meant Ryan needed seven groomsmen. For some reason we couldn't get one spot on the groomsmen's side filled. One would commit and then something would come up and he couldn't do it. This went on up until a few weeks before the wedding when we finally just had to throw in the towel and only have six groomsmen and seven bridesmaids. I did not realize how much things being off centered bothered me until this problem arose. I knew it bothered me some but now that my wedding party wasn't the same amount of people on one side as it was on the other, it would be a tough battle in my brain to overcome. I did eventually though and one groomsman ended up walking out with a bridesmaid on each arm and I can assure you that he wasn't complaining and that was not at all a problem for him.

After we finally got the final wedding party figured out, it was time to start planning a bachelor and bachelorette party. For weeks we went back and forth on what we all wanted to do and our final decision was to go out separately but on the same night in downtown Nashville, TN. I could probably come up with an entire piece of notebook paper worth of a list as to why this wasn't a good idea. Both the bridesmaids and the groomsmen booked rooms in two different hotels about fifteen blocks apart. As the wedding approached, so did this night out on the town and at this point, we could hardly contain our excitement.

Separately, we all packed our things and hit the road to go stay the night in Nashville and celebrate the last fling before the ring. When I say this was a night to remember, I mean it. This whole night could have been made into a movie. The girls started off at a bar that the boot company I work for had tight connections with. We would basically bar hop all night and just really soak up and enjoy this very rare girl's night out together. I'm not one to seek much attention and most definitely not in front of a big crowd, note how I said that I wasn't a fan of public speaking. Well, this night required me to stick out. I wore a veil that existed on a tiara that they girls bought for me to wear. At one of the bars it was suggested that I get up on the bar and take a shot with all off my bridesmaids. Well, first of all I don't take shots and second of all, this just wasn't my style to be honest. As usual though, get a little bit of alcohol in anyone and you may be able to convince them to do things they would usually be too shy to do. We really had a great night together. We danced, laughed, and made awesome memories of what would personally be my only night out in Nashville bar hopping. I can count on one hand all of bar nights I've had and I can assure you, those were enough.

So here we are having an awesome time together and one of my friends accidentally lost the battery to her phone while we were dancing at the previous bar. She and I, and another friend took off to find it and somehow information got misconstrued and before you knew it, Ryan had gotten a phone call that I was missing. In the midst of the phone battery hunt we had going, we had found a lady on the side of the road who had no doubt seen better days. Someone had called a cab for her because she had gone well past her limit of alcohol consumption but she couldn't get into the cab because she couldn't stand. My other two girlfriends and I helped get her into the cab so she could be taken home. Of course we had no idea that a search party was underway for me because no one realized I had been included in the mission of locating the battery for my friend's phone. By this point, I had lost my phone, my one friend was missing the battery to her phone that we never found, and the other member of the search party, her phone was dead.

Of course when we got back with the other girls, the guys had already met up with them and everyone was in such panic thinking I was missing. After a scuffle with a few of the bouncers and some of the groomsmen, we finally headed back to the hotel rooms. One of my favorite parts of this entire story is that in three separate hotel rooms, Clarksville brought coed sleepovers to downtown Nashville. The boys had a hotel room and the girls had two hotel rooms but by the end of the night, that didn't matter at all.

We would spend our next week prepping for the wedding and doing last minute, mandatory tasks that were required for everything to come together smoothly. I had an incredibly helpful bridal party so they made so many things easier for me. That's the best thing about having genuine friends is that they will help you in any way that they can. I took the day before and the day of off of work to spend time at the venue decorating and setting up. At last, November 11, 2011 was here and it was time to marry my high school sweetheart.

Because November 11th is Veterans Day, a lot of people already had the day off. It was a Friday so we did the wedding in the evening time. Ryan didn't want to get married at a church and I respected that so we got married at the venue we had planned to do the reception at and it worked out just fine. Wedding days always seems so rushed. All of this prepping and planning you've done over the past year, comes to pass in just a few hours but it's always worth all of the hard work and effort, at least mine was.

I love nothing more than having everyone I love in one place. Rather it's friends or family or both all together it is extremely fulfilling to my heart. What better place than my own wedding to have all of these people I love all together. The evening of November 11, 2011 was a dream come true. I finally got to marry the man that had my heart for the past eight years.

All of the groomsmen were on one side of the venue getting ready and all of the bridesmaids were on the other. Everyone was super hyped up and pumped for our big night. I can't necessarily speak for our friends but if I had to guess, I would say they were just as excited to see us get married as we were to finally be getting married. I could see it in their smiles and feel it in their energy. All of the guys were in the kitchen helping prep food for our catering lady who worked her tail off to be sure all of the food was perfect. All of the girls were in the room with me helping me get all prepped and zipped up. My photographer captured a photo of one of my bridesmaids putting my heels on my feet. I knew no one would see my feet because of the length of my dress, so a pedicure didn't make the cut when it came to the wedding budget. When that picture showed up in the captured photos line up with a half painted big toe, I second guessed that budget decision, only for a moment though. Another picture captured was all of the bridesmaids standing behind me with two long ribbons pulled completely out that hung down on the back of my dress. This picture was captured right before they laced up the back of my dress. This moment occurred shortly before I walked out.

I decided to have my grandfather and mom's boyfriend Patrick walk me half way down the aisle to give me to my dad and then my dad walk me to Ryan to give me away. Patrick had been in my life for about ten years at this point and had really been a huge influence in my life. He had been so helpful with mom and did so much for the two of us that I felt it was necessary to involve him in some way. Papa was a big influence in my life as well. I am his only grandchild and he was always sure to help me in any way that he could if I needed him to even though it was always scary asking him. He just so happens to be the same grandfather that I described earlier as being frugal. It was always a last resort situation getting him involved but the important point is that he was always there.

Patrick and Papa walked me half way down to my dad and my dad took me up to the altar with Ryan, who in about ten minutes would be my husband. I was so nervous! I am not at all a fan of standing up in front a crowded room, even if I know every individual in there and I have to say very few words. At one point I thought I was going to faint or get sick. The urge came within me to just run to the door. I'm not sure where or when this originated in me because it felt like it came out of nowhere but I have a true fear of feeling stuck. I'm not a fan of elevators. I'm not a fan of flying. I'm not a fan of any moment that I feel stuck in. Of course if I process the entire thought instead of immediately feeling stuck in a stuck moment, I would be fine. For instance, it was my wedding. If I absolutely had to take off running out of the building for any reason at all, I could have. If anything it would have made it even more memorable for my guest. The only thing that stopped me from realizing that is my panic and fear. I wouldn't allow my brain to finish that thought. Same thing with an elevator situation, if I get stuck in there, someone will eventually come rescue me.

We exchanged our vows and we each had our own vase which had two different color sands in them. This is best comparable to the candle lighting ceremony at a traditional wedding, but this sand moment was new and we preferred that for ours. The idea was for each of us to pour the sand into a jar together and the end result would look like what I can only describe as looking like inside the jar would be swirled with two different colors. While it never occurred to me that this specific part could go any other way than the way I had imagined, it did. When we got done pouring our sand, the pastor requested that we shake the jar that we had both just poured our sand vases into, together. This made for a memorable moment for me. No one else realized it wasn't supposed to happen that way and that we should not have shook the sand jar so I took a deep breath and let it go.

"I now pronounce you husband and wife, you may now kiss your bride." Those words came shortly after the failed sand moment and I had forgotten all about the sand situation when that kiss happened. I was officially married to my boyfriend of eight years and it was time to celebrate with all of our supporters! The whole wedding party formally exited the ceremony area and we all headed to take pictures outside while everyone enjoyed the delicious food that our lovely groomsmen helped with.

When we came back in from what felt like hours of photography, it was time for the father daughter dance. A precious and lasting moment I will never forget. My dad and I had always kept in contact but of course we weren't as close and my mom and I were. I had lived with my mom my entire life and only visited dad on the weekends. Because of this, it didn't leave an incredibly large amount of bonding time for my dad and I. Growing up I had always admired my dad for the God loving man that he was. He was a hero if I had ever seen one. My dad had overcome a brain aneurism and also a brain tumor within years apart. Not many people could see the cape I saw hanging from his shoulders that night we danced together. That's one of the most special moments I cherish the most from that evening.

Speaking of special moments, Ryan and I had one for the books for a wedding night. As our guest started to slowly call it a night and leave, we all kind of migrated outside to the parking lot. As Ryan and I packed the truck up for when we would depart for our honeymoon suite shortly, we both just so happened to glance up to the sky at the same time and see a shooting star. How special was that? All of these people who stood outside with us never even saw it, only me and Ryan. What a perfect ending to a perfect day. The rest was history.

5

He Strengthens Us

In the weeks to come, the topic of house purchasing would resurface. It was really hard for me but I kept reminding myself that this was supposed to happen. I was supposed to leave the nest and start a life of my own. The back of my mind kept telling me that if I did that, mom would have no one. This time in my life was pretty tough on me. In the mean time I had a pregnancy test show up positive. It wasn't just one test that showed positive, but three. This would help ease the heartache I would experience with leaving mom. This baby would help her hopefully refrain from overtaking her medication. This baby could be the reason that she could call herself sober. All of these thoughts came rushing in just as quickly as my heart sank at the appointment that there wasn't a heartbeat. Devastated was an understatement.

A few months later, Ryan and I found a house and put an offer in on it and it was set to close May 10, 2012. In the meantime, we had more pregnancy tests show up positive. Again, mom went with me to the doctor where we got an ultrasound and a heartbeat. This was fantastic! We had a baby on the way to help distract us all from the big change that was coming. Mom and I were being separated after twenty-four years of spending our lives together at this was a big deal.

I know this may seem so stretched but it was really this serious for us. Our bond was so incredibly special. She was my best friend and the bond we shared was something I can only hope every child gets to experience with their mom. Well, the side of the bond without the addiction. I think it's probably most little girl's dream to have a relationship with their mom like my mom and I had. If you had asked any of my girl friends over the years if they wished they had a bond with their mom like I do mine, I'm sure they would tell you yes.

Within two weeks of closing on our first home, a trip to the bathroom would again leave us feeling hopeless. Packing and moving kept us distracted from another painful loss. There is nothing quite like getting your hopes up for something you have looked forward to for so long, only to watch all of the plans you've made for the new baby's room fall apart.

Ryan and I still found ways to enjoy ourselves in our new home like coming home from work and cuddling on our couch binge watching TV shows together. We would have friends come over every weekend and we would all drink responsibly of course and just have a good time together. At our new house we had a detached garage and off to the side of the garage part there was a twenty foot by twelve foot room that was perfect for studio purposes for him. He built a booth in there and sound proofed not only the booth but the whole area. It was legit in there. By doing this, it was easier for the men to convince us ladies to join them out there. Those were some really good times!

Since we moved out of moms, papa thought it would be a good idea for her to downsize to something smaller. He owned that house so he planned to sell that one and put her in a new one. She went from a three bedroom, two and a half bathrooms with a basement home to a two bedroom and one bathroom home. It was perfect for her though and she loved it. She seemed so ecstatic for the change. She was so excited to get in this new home and make new memories. It was a fresh start. By the beginning of November of 2012, she was all moved in and the old house was put up for auction, per papa's choice. I guess to him that seemed it would be the easiest way to get rid of it. He had complained about it since day one because he had taken over the payments on it and bought it outright eventually, shortly after her and my step-dad had gotten divorced.

We did Thanksgiving at our new house. I cooked for mom, papa, and her surviving older brother who I call Bub. It was different cooking for them here because I had cooked for them for so long at the other house on the holidays but change is good I suppose. I had planned to do the same for Christmas but mom said she wasn't feeling good that day which wasn't out of the ordinary so I went to her that Christmas. I say it wasn't out of the ordinary for

45

mom to not feel good because she struggled with other things amongst addiction. She was born with spinal bifida so she struggled a lot with pain. She also struggled a lot with depression and anxiety so it was always a big task to get her out to go somewhere. I think more than anything, the addiction was to sooth not only mental pain but also physical pain. I would hate to never feel good physically, emotionally, or mentally so I can't even imagine how she really felt. I couldn't have empathy for her because I had never really experienced any of those things but I always had compassion for her. That was one of her best assets for herself that she passed down to me, compassion.

The holidays were always tough for her because holidays are never the same once you lose someone you love that you shared those holiday memories with. Her heartache never really seemed to ease until after January passed. January was always a tough month for her because her mom passed away on January 18. January of 2013 was different though.

Mom had some teeth pulled the first week of January and she was so excited for this. She was finally getting some dentures that she had never had the money to afford in the past. She had come across an opportunity to finally purchase these and I had not seen her look forward to something as much as she did this, in a very long time. The quality of teeth in each person is hereditary and unfortunately she had been passed down her daddy's teeth. Of course as a retired military man who had served in Vietnam and his lifestyle of being overly frugal, his appearance wasn't necessarily something he worried about. For a woman who had it all together for so many years and worked with the public her entire work history, appearance was everything so as you can imagine, this was devastating to her. I think that's where quite a bit of her social anxiety came from also. She didn't even feel comfortable smiling and honestly, it was rare I ever saw her smile because of this. She developed a complex about it and it broke my heart to see her so broken from it.

On January 10, I was over at my best friend's house and I called to check on mom. It was normal for us to talk at least twice a day but with her teeth being pulled, I had not really gotten to talk to her as much over the past week. She spent a lot of time sleeping which I'm sure is the most peaceful way to recover from a dental procedure because mouth pain is the worst and if you're asleep, you don't have to feel it. It was the sweetest conversation. We were trying to get my best friends precious two year old to get on the phone and talk to mom, but she was being bashful. This Thursday evening phone call was pretty special to me. Mom and I said our goodbyes and told each other we loved each other and I told her I would call and check on her the next day.

Friday came and I attempted calling her all day but I couldn't get her to pick up the phone. It wasn't unusual for her to miss a call, especially during the recent week. Because of her history with medication and having a tendency to take too many pills, I had an agreement with her that I would not come over there if she didn't pick up the phone. I never wanted to walk in on something devastating. I hated that I thought like this but I'm telling you, addiction and the situations it causes are traumatizing. The state of mind or lack thereof that I had found her in, in the past, were enough to leave a scar big enough to prevent me from showing up if I hadn't spoke to her. That alone should speak for its self. Through this entire addiction battle she had that I sometimes felt as if I fought harder for her than she did, my brain was wired to always expect the worst and it controlled me.

I had asked her boyfriend, Patrick if he would go by and check on her Saturday since she never answered for me on Friday and he said he didn't mind and that he would. He didn't tell me a time that he planned on going by there so I went ahead and headed off to do my routine Saturday grocery shopping. I thought it was so cool because on this particular Saturday, I saw my favorite teacher from high-school for the first time since I graduated which had been six and a half years prior and oddly enough, I haven't seen her since! I was so excited to see her and catch up. I had thought of her so often since I left high-school. I had often wondered if she still worked there and if they would let me come in the school and visit her. I had also searched for her on social media periodically but never had any luck. This should give you an idea of how excited I was to see her and catch up with her that day.

48

I had two more isles to go when I got a call from Patrick. I thought I would finish out my shopping and then call him back once I got to the car just in case something was wrong. A minute went by and he called back again. It wasn't unusual for Patrick to call back to back so I made my way to the checkout line and as I stood there, he called again. That third phone call left me with a thought that I continued tried to push out of my head and a feeling that I had never felt until that day and I pray I never have to feel again. I kept reciting in my head, "Hold it together." Panic sank in. I'm sure the cashier had no idea that in that moment, my brain looked like a computer hard drive being exhausted with information and the inside of my body felt like it was experiencing an earthquake. I took a lot of deep breaths as I swiftly headed to my car. On the way to the car, Patrick called again. At this point I started running and I couldn't hide the tremors my body was experiencing on the inside. I started throwing, literally throwing all of my groceries into the car. I used all of this uncontrollable adrenaline caused energy, to push my cart into the cart return so that there was no chance it could roll back out because I had to sit down immediately. I had to get back to my car.

It was so weird because as much as my brain kept trying to convince me of the worst case scenario as it usually did, my gut for the first time, confirmed it. As I sat there and pushed Patrick's name on my missed calls list, my heart could probably be seen beating from outside of my chest. When Patrick answered the phone, he was crying. Through the tears and a very distinctive muffled voice that I will never forget, all he could say was, "Beck's gone." For about two minutes, which felt like two hours, I debated on calling an ambulance for myself because I could not breathe. It felt like my chest had shrunk in half and I could not catch my breath. My heart was beating so hard that it literally took my breath away. I felt lifeless. I could not move. My best friend in the entire world that I tried so hard to save from this very moment was gone.

I immediately hung up with Patrick and called Ryan to come and get me. I could hardly function at this point. I wasn't sobbing but I was shaking so much that my insides were shaking. I was in complete shock. When Ryan picked up the phone all I could find the words to say were, "Mom is gone. Can you please come get me?" If I could put the way he responded verbally into writing his, "What?" was capitalized, underlined, and had an unlimited amount of exclamation marks and question marks. He said he was on his way and luckily we only lived about five minutes away from the grocery store. As I sat and waited for him I called my dad and my closest friends to let them know what was going on. Every single person's response was exactly the same as Ryan's. When Ryan arrived, we left his truck at the grocery store and he drove my car to my mom's.

If a specific moment could be lived twice in one life, this particular moment was it. As we turned the corner to turn on the road that led to mom's house, the same feeling that sank my heart in 2006 when we turned the corner to my uncle Michael's, was painfully being experienced again. Yellow tape surrounded her house and numerous emergency vehicles and police cars lined the street. My appearance from the outside was somber but what existed on the inside was pure chaos. This had to be a dream and someone needed to wake me up.

We didn't stay long because her body was still inside and everything including the premises itself was under investigation. They really didn't want us on the property just in case it was a homicide case. Patrick was being held there and questioned since he was the one that found her. None of it felt right but I'm sure it's protocol for any situation when there has been a death.

Mom had a fourteen year old Jack Russell Terrier named Josie who would not quit barking. If you have ever seen this breed of dog would know that she was no more than fifteen pounds soaking wet but this day she acted as if she was a one-hundred pound vicious guard dog. She was barking at and trying to bite every officer that went in to the house. She was protecting what she had always known as her best friend. If I had to guess where Josie was when Patrick walked in and found mom deceased in her bed, I would guess that Josie was right there next to mom.

Ryan and I got Josie and left. We went home and unloaded all of our groceries before they were ruined. It was barely spitting snow that day and was overcast. The way it felt outside was exactly how I felt on the inside, gloomy and grey. I remember I wasn't even wearing a jacket because of how hot the inside of my body was. When adrenaline is at its highest, it sure can put off some heat.

If there was one thing certain about Ryan and me, it was our friendships. We had a very big, loving group of friends and they all called my mom, "Mama" because she was that for every one. Throughout the remainder of that day, friends would show up randomly and by nightfall, we had a house full of them. One of the things I miss the most about the, "Good ole days" is our friends, and the routine we had in spending every weekend together.

I had never arranged or planned a funeral before and honestly I had never even thought about it, but I suppose there's a first time for everything. The next day I called and made an appointment at the funeral home. I went to the funeral home to discuss the arrangements and we sat at this big table that could have sat eight people the only people that were in there were me and my grandfather. I couldn't help but to feel heartbroken for him because this sadly was the second funeral he would be paying for and planning for one of his children. We walked around and looked at caskets and finally decided on one together. You don't think about these things on a daily basis but not only do you purchase a casket for someone who is deceased, you also purchase a vault. The casket is placed in the vault which is a humongous empty box at the burial site. They use vaults to completely seal everything off. It helps to preserve the body.

I remember experiencing a lot of uncomfortable decisions I had to make during the planning period as well. I had to decide what clothing she would be wearing in the casket for the visitation. Would I want her to wear shoes or no shoes? I had to decide if I wanted her to wear the skirt part of the outfit since no one could see it and they could only see from the top to her waist. My mom was very modest so I could not let that woman be buried without her skirt on. I had to decide what jewelry she would wear. Would I want to take the jewelry off and keep it after the visitation or would I want her to be buried in it? I had to have a hair stylist come in and style her hair. I debated on having them paint her nails but decided against it. She had just recently painted them soft lavender purple. It was a new polish she had gotten which oddly enough I still have. There are some things you just don't know how to let go of when someone you love dies.

The next few days altogether are a blur but the feeling I felt in the moments I experienced are unforgettable. I decided to have her dressed in the outfit she wore to my wedding. Her and I went and picked that out together. She looked as beautiful in it then as she did the day she tried it on when we went shopping. We decided on a four hour visitation the first day and then a two hour visitation before the funeral the next day. I don't know how many people I talked to or how many people I met for the first time but I do know that my mom was deeply loved. I sat up at the casket every minute of visitation time and I don't think I cried once. I couldn't feel anything at all. The only thing I was very sure I felt was emptiness.

The preacher did a great job during the service. He read a eulogy that I wrote for her which made me cry harder hearing it than it did writing it. Our bond was complicated because of her addiction, but it was beautiful and that's the picture it painted in the words I wrote for her. Her funeral was followed by a short graveside service that more than half of the people who attended her funeral, attended. I remember sitting under the tent they set up for family at the grave site and looking back at all the people there, realizing how truly loved she was and also recognizing her impact. Her impact to every life she had touched was unforgettable. That was her gift, love.

6

When We Are Weary

He Provides

My grandfather being the frugal man he is wanted the house he had recently put her in, to be cleaned out pronto. That process was tough and honestly felt somewhat unfair. Here I was being rushed to go through everything that she had and then had to decide rather it was coming with me, getting donated, or getting tossed in the trash. I couldn't comment much because the house was owned by him and he wanted it rented or sold as soon as it could be so I worked as quickly as I could. Looking back, it was probably more of a blessing than unfair, because there's no telling how long it may have sat there untouched if given that opportunity. It's really hard to let go of a loved one's items like that.

God love her soul, she kept everything. She was one of those people who just couldn't let go of the things she was forced to take when loved ones of hers had passed away. Imagine a two story, three bedroom home with a garage getting stuffed into a one story two bedroom home with no garage. Let me remind you that she had just moved, so a lot of these things were just piled around waiting for a permanent home in the house. Now imagine going through all of that. I thankfully had quite a bit of help so that made it a little easier.

We finally got her house cleaned out within about two weeks and my grandfather sold it. Now what? What's next for me? What is next for my life after such a painful and tragic loss? Other than my job, I didn't really have anything else to be responsible for now that she was gone. She was my responsibility. She was my purpose, so to say, and in the blink of an eye, that changed.

Before I knew it, I found myself drinking quite a bit. It wasn't a typical two to three drinks; it was five, six, and seven. Fifty percent of the time I was blacking out. It wasn't a healthy lifestyle at all. I specifically remember driving to work on Monday thinking, "I shouldn't even be driving right now" because I was still buzzing from the night before. It was a Monday, y'all. I don't know if you have ever been at a point in your life when you felt this low before but one thing I have realized through all of the ups and downs in life is that in my highest of highs and lowest if lows, God has always been there.

I remember I would leave home and go with my girlfriends every chance I got. I did the best I could to avoid home. I spent every spare moment I could avoiding reality. At that point in my life I had convinced myself that if I just got rid of my life prior to her death and started a new life, everything would be okay. No matter how brave I felt like I was to take this next step and start a new life, I never could do it. I am so incredibly thankful that God was there with me in my lowest of lows because I would not have the amazing and beautiful life that I have today if I had just threw away everything I had ever known. Thank God that chapter of my life was cut short by His greater plan.

On December 31, 2013, I shared with the public that Ryan and I were expecting. I had finally made it past the nine week point and felt completely comfortable with sharing our exciting news with everyone. I was so thankful that God had gifted me with this because it wasn't only a want at this point, but a desperate need. The due date was July 14, 2014. I needed something to help me get through the loss of my mom. I needed something to help mend my broken heart.

Shortly after I had announced this, I headed back for a routine doctor visit only hear the heart wrenching words I had heard twice before, "There is not a heartbeat." Here it was February and I was thinking I was twelve weeks pregnant at this point only to be told I'm caring a baby that no longer carries a heartbeat. Let me share with you that nothing in this world has made me feel more useless than not being able to carry a child. Every single miscarriage made me feel so insignificant. Every single time I always looked directly at myself and wondered what in the world is wrong with me? Why can't I do this? Why can't my body create a life? What am I doing wrong? If there's nothing else in this world that makes you question things, rest assured, having three miscarriages in a row will.

They didn't waste any time and got me right in within the next week to have a D & C done. I hadn't been far enough along to have to have this procedure done previously so this was all new to me. There were a lot of emotions that existed between the time I heard the words, "There is not a heartbeat" and the moment I woke up from the anesthesia from having the D & C done. They ranged from, "Can we check one more time for a heartbeat before we do this?" to "Let's just get this over with and be done with it." The emotions that came from this were always so draining. Ryan and I both just felt like throwing our hands up in the air. We both had definitely gotten to a point that we were scared to even get excited about pregnancy anymore.

The D & C was a scary process for me and was more emotional for me than it may have been for most. You see, one of my mom's greatest assets was compassion. She just had that naturally in her to care for others. She was the best nurse a daughter could ever pray for. My mom had come to basically all of my doctor's appointments with me all the way up until the day she died. Even after I moved out, if I was sick, she would pick me up and take me to the doctor. Remember, I was twenty-four years old when I moved out. Yes, she sure would come pick her baby up and carry her to the doctor if she didn't feel good. So you can only imagine how much compassion I was missing from her while experiencing something so scary for the first time. I had never had anesthesia and I had never had any type of surgery. Plus I was already heartbroken from my third miscarriage and the fact I didn't have my mom there to give the type of love that only moms can give. I was a complete mess needless to say.

Thank God for a fantastic, irreplaceable group of friends who have stood by my side and have loved me through all of it. When I got home that day they had brought me a sweet little stuffed zebra, with my favorite chocolate bars, a card, and a precious friendship book. It was such a thoughtful thing for them to do and it was definitely something I needed that day. The only person that knew I was experiencing all of those emotions and feelings was me, so they will never really know how much that simple gesture meant to me that day.

Back to the drinking I went. This just added more emotion to my life that felt so empty so bottle after bottle I consumed. My two very best friends were getting married in May so that meant two bachelorette parties and two wedding to be in. There, I had something to look forward to. I had a few more purposes to fulfill in the upcoming future. The person I was experiencing within myself at that point in my life was ready to throw down and do some partying.

Thank God for my loving husband. He's never been controlling or the type to tell me no to something that I wanted to do although looking back, I wouldn't have blamed him if he had been and in a way, I kind of wish he was because I needed it at that particular point in my life. He just put up with me. It's like he would give me an inch and I would take a mile. I'll use my best friend's bachelorette night for example. I was going to be responsible for the first time in a while and be the designated driver for my best friend and another friend of ours. I would drive them to their home at the end of our night and I would return home sober with my car. We rented a limo for the beginning of the shindig so we had already planned accordingly and had my car at the bar that we intended to end our night at. That way at the end of the night we could just hop in my car and I could drive everyone home safely.

I don't know if you have ever been with a group of fifteen ladies celebrating your friend's bachelorette night but let's just say the ending was quite a bit different than what I had told my husband. Basically, one drink led to another and another friend of ours who was actually responsible ended up driving my car and got us all home safely. That was hard explaining the next morning. What was even harder was knowing that I had let him down and didn't hold up my end of the deal. Again, thank God for my loving husband who put up with me and never let his love waiver through this confused and painful time in my life.

From February to May, I had been back and forth to the doctor as they tried to figure out what could be going on and why I wasn't able to carry a child completely through the first trimester. Through doing this we found out that I had hypothyroidism which at the time I didn't realize could be the major reason behind the miscarriages. Our thyroid does a lot more for our body than we realize. It actually provides quite a bit to a baby and is a very important resource the entire first trimester of a pregnancy. I remember specifically being sent to a specialist in Nashville and during that appointment, I just had a feeling that I was pregnant again. I didn't say anything though because I just didn't want to know at this point. I was scared of being let down if I wasn't pregnant and I was scared to know if I was because, it would have been natural for me to have that fearful feeling of another possible loss.

May 13, 2014 I took a pregnancy test that confirmed my fourth pregnancy. Ryan and I were stoked but so dang nervous. We felt so good about this one because we had all the right medications to make it happen. My thyroid was producing everything it was supposed to be with the help of medication. I had been prescribed extra folic acid by the specialist that would also help carry the baby through the first trimester and also the remainder of the pregnancy. Because of my medical history, they scheduled me for an ultrasound more often than most expectant mothers just as an extra precaution. We were going to wait to announce it this time. We were planning to announce it once we found out the gender at sixteen weeks.

It was so hard to contain our excitement. We wanted to shout it from rooftops and tell everyone we passed at the supermarket. We were ecstatic, especially after we made it past week twelve. Shortly after Ryan's birthday in July, we walked in that ultrasound room so anxious. We weren't sure if we were going to be brining in a baby Ryan or a baby Kristen. We both were team boy. I honestly didn't care either way but Ryan wanted a boy so bad, so I just backed him with that wish. Right off the ultrasound tech's lips rolled, "It's a GIRL." Neither of us was disappointed obviously because we both just desperately wanted to be parents at this point. We had our pictures made that day, girl themed, and already had her name picked out, Laney, our precious angel.

The next few months we would do all the things most people do before having a baby. We got her a crib and furniture to match. We painted her room pink, grey, and white. Her daddy sure did put a lot of precious time into that beautiful room he created for her. We had everything in place and all her sweet little baby clothes washed. All we were waiting on at this point was her.

Those last few months of pregnancy were so precious to me. She was so active and my most favorite thing to do was to go home, prop my feet up, and Ryan and I would just sit there and watch her in full action. It always made us giggle to see her get the hiccups in there too. She was pretty entertaining to watch. We would set something on my belly and she would kick and roll around until she knocked it off. We thoroughly enjoyed this part.

The thought of her having to exit out of that belly that she constantly performed gymnastics in is where most of my anxiety stepped in. One of my biggest fears of my entire adulthood at this point was giving birth. The thought of it made my heart sink. I've learned though the only way to overcome a fear is to conquer it and with this fear, I didn't have a choice. This would be another emotional moment for me because I didn't have my mom's compassionate personality there to comfort me in ways only mom can, so I thought. Laney's due date was January 8th, 2015 but toward the very end of my pregnancy, I started swelling so my doctor went ahead and scheduled an induction for December 31st, 2014. This kind of worked out in my favor anyways for two reasons. One reason was because I was super terrified but had an amazing doctor who I knew would help me feel comfortable and knew for sure she would be there for the delivery that day if she scheduled me for an induction. The other reason was that the date of my mom's death is January 12th and I just wasn't sure how I would feel if Laney was born that day or days close to that day. It would all work out best for everyone with a scheduled induction, so December 31st and Laney were all we were waiting for at this point.

7

My Sunshine

The night before, I remember being in her bedroom looking at my big belly thinking, "I get to meet you tomorrow." Over time I have developed a way of really trying to be present in a moment and I specifically remember thinking, "This is mine and my husband's last night of it being just us." At this point, we had been together for eleven years so this was going to be a huge change, but a wonderful one to say the least. I don't know if I even truly slept that night honestly. Between being anxious and excited and then factoring in the fact I was too big to get comfortable enough to even relax long enough to sleep, I'd assume I didn't.

We had to be at the hospital at 5 a.m. that morning. Ryan and I walked in, hand in hand without any idea what all our day entailed or the experiences we would encounter. All that we knew is that we were there to have a baby. We met with a lady in the registering department that got us all checked in and sent us on our merry way up to our room. I kept hoping someone would walk in and say, "Okay, this is how it's going to happen. She will be here at this time. It will most likely take this long." But as we all know, no one knows what the future holds, no matter who we are. I was so scared. There was so much unknown at this time.

I put on that lovely hospital gown that everyone is always so excited to put on when they have to stay at the hospital. There is no doubt in my mind that whoever designed that thing was pretty carefree. You have to be to be wearing that thing around! It was designed for people with a lot of confidence and for sure by someone who was unfamiliar with the quote, "Modest is hottest." Someone needs to do something about that paper thin piece of material that they encourage you to wear. I mean, we pay enough while we're there for something a little more comfortable, am I right?

The nurse came in and put a band with a piece of equipment connected to it around my belly that detected Laney's heart rate. There was a machine right next to the bed that constantly printed off paper with the history of my contractions which also required machine hook up. I was only dilated to a one at this pint so needless to say we had a long day ahead of us if that was any indication of the future. At about 9 a.m. a doctor came in and broke my water so that we could finally get this process stared. There is a type of liquid that they give to help jump start the labor process and it is called pitocin. They came and hung this on the IV pole along with an IV and back to the wait we went. The nurse told me to tell her when I started feeling contractions and that when I did, they would come and give me the epidural.

By noon, I had my epidural and was dilated to a three. I had made it through my whole pregnancy without throwing up but the pain I felt shortly after they put my epidural in, was about to make me to get sick. The pain I was feeling was terrible. What had happened was that my epidural had somehow come out of my spine so I was feeling every bit of everything. Now, at this point I was still dilated to a three so my tolerance for physical pain I found out that day is pretty low. There are mom's who get all the way dilated to a ten with back to back contractions and do it without that epidural. To all of you mom's out there who do it naturally, you are the real MVP. We all have our own strengths and weaknesses. Childbirth without an epidural is not my strength. Until they could get the lady back in there to put a new epidural in, they gave me a cold rag and ice chips. I don't think I'm being dramatic when I say it was probably about two hours of this pain.

I had visitors throughout the day but now it was about 5 p.m. and I had a room full of people staying until Laney made her debut. In the room was Ryan, who stayed at my bedside basically the whole day, my dad, my step-mom, my little brother, and three of my very close friends who came when they got off work. They were all so supportive and were just as anxious for her arrival as I was. We had all, together, been waiting for this moment for years.

In the midst of all of this happening and the pain I was experiencing, I remember one very special moment that I will never forget. I didn't really think as much about my mom not being there as I thought I would. It is hard to be sad about someone being absent from something that is so joyful and exciting. I had a few moments but I was emotional about everything that day so this next moment really stayed with me. My friends that were there to witness it deemed it as special as I did. My dad got up from the couch and walked over to me and started rubbing my head very gently and told me how much he loved me and how proud of me that he was. He stayed there for a good full minute and then softly kissed my forehead and went and sat back down. Bless his heart, he felt so helpless. I can't imagine seeing my daughter in a lot of pain and not being able to take it away for her. My dad had always been a gentle and loving type of man so it came as no surprise when he did this, but the way it made me feel on such an emotional day, in such a painful moment, was unforgettable. I will always cherish that moment and hold it near and dear to my heart.

The lady finally came back and inserted the second epidural and it worked like a charm. It was about 6pm now and I was still only dilated to a three. What I did not know at 6 p.m. is that at 7 p.m. there would be a shift change and I would end up with the sweetest nurse in the hospital. If she had a quote she used as to how she approached my labor process it would be, "Let's bring this baby into the world now." She came in that room, turned up my pitocin, and within no time I was dilated to a four. By 9:30 p.m. I was dilated to a ten and we were ready for action. My dad, step-mom, and brother all left the room. Ryan and three of my greatest friend stayed din there with me. It was go time and Ryan looked as nervous about it as I felt. Thankfully, my girlfriends that stayed in there with me, had all given birth before so they knew what was normal and what was not. Typically they offer a mirror for you to watch if you want to but I don't do well with the type of situation that was about to occur. I watched my friend's facial expressions and would occasionally look at the reflection that the delivery nurse's glasses were showing. That's how I kept up with the delivery situation.

At 10:26pm, here came the most beautiful girl in the universe. She had these big blue eyes and the most precious set of lips. She had a head full of dark hair and a sweet little button nose. All of the things that concerned me were quickly explained by my girlfriends who had been there done that. Laney's head was oval in shape which was from being in the birth canal for a little while. Her precious skin was purple tinted in color which eventually went away after an hour or two. She was so quiet. You see all of these movies and hear all of these stories about babies clearing out their lungs by crying, like screaming crying, and she wasn't doing that at all. My doctor answered questions to everything I was concerned about and reassured me that my precious angel was fine.

As soon as she came out, right before they took her to weigh her and clean her off, they placed her in my arms. There aren't enough words available to describe that moment for me. Life had never been more perfect and God had never made me feel so special to have been blessed with such a perfectly beautiful, healthy baby girl. Even though everything else around me operated, everything in me stood still. This little angel is exactly what I needed. I felt complete.

They took her from my arms and laid her in the basinet. They turned on that little heat lamp that she was not happy about at all. They started sucking all of the fluid out of her mouth and her nose with one of those little sucker devices. Meanwhile, there her daddy stood right there beside her in complete amazement. He will never know what my view of that moment was. We finally had our precious baby that we had prayed for, for years. We had our own little family.

We got released two days later and home we went with our new bundle of joy. It was such a cool and memorable experience for Ryan and me to take on all of these challenges together for the first time. One of the biggest fears as parents to a newborn is that the baby will just stop breathing. For about the first three nights, Ryan and I slept in shifts. Whoever was awake would watch her to make sure she was breathing while the other one slept for a few hours. Take note from two experienced parents, sleep when the baby sleeps. This process will not hold up.

Post partum depression is a frequently talked about term after giving birth. I think the majority of this type of depression shows up because of such a big shock having a baby causes to your life. New moms and dads aren't given a manual on how to be parents. You can't rent a nurse to come home with you when you bring the new baby home. There is so much abrupt change after having a baby that it is almost too much to take in at one time. Life as you knew it is completely different and for anyone experiencing being a mom for the very first time, it is intense.

I was never clinically diagnosed with post partum depression but I definitely believe I experienced some. Deep within I was also experiencing quite a bit of emotion about doing this without my mom there to help me. She had every answer I needed except she wasn't present to answer my questions. Also, Laney would never get to know her. Mom would have been an amazing meme to her. Mom was going to miss out on the most special thing I had ever experienced. It was so tough the first couple of months. Again, thank God for great friends who were already moms and were very educated in the baby department. They helped me through some of the hardest days.

Prior to this new mom life, I never slept in late. I wasn't a big sleeper like some people tend to be so I was going to be a pro at getting up with her. I slept until maybe 8am on the weekends so this whole waking up to a baby was going to be a breeze. I remember thinking of how Ryan not only slept in late, but is also a deep sleeper so I would go ahead and count him out for the waking up with the baby duty which was totally fine with me. If any mom had been able to witness this thinking process going through my brain, they would have really enjoyed this comical theory I had. In all seriousness, this is not at all how it works and the joke was on this momma.

It never crossed my mind that I had never been woken up in the middle of sleep numerous times throughout a night. Let me be clear when I say there is a huge difference in not being a big sleeper and in not sleeping in on the weekends, and being woken up in the middle of sleep. They cannot be compared. This would become one of the most emotional things I would experience. I am a pretty cheerful and positive person and most of the time I can be found full of joy and with a smile. I did not realize until this point in my life that perhaps sleep was very important to me and when I was woken up during sleep, I could not be found cheerful. Joy was not a word that I would use to describe me. It was actually the complete opposite.

In the heat of a moment, we feel justified and we feel as if we have credible reasoning for behaving specific ways so we go ahead and go all the way through with the action that our emotions prompt. These moments would come for me in the middle of the night. As soon as I got out of the bed I'd stomp around and huff and puff. I'd complain about how I wish she would just sleep through the night. What in the world could she possibly need now?

I just changed her and gave her a bottle. Well hello Kristen, this is what you prayed for though.

Even to this day if I am tired, it's simple, I'm emotional. I think most every human can relate to this. I will respond to things completely different when I'm exhausted than I will when I am on my second cup of coffee in the morning. A good, strengthened, healthy state of mind happens when we get enough rest. The first few months it was nearly impossible to achieve this but after she was about three months old, she was only waking up one time throughout the night. By this point I was able to get enough rest to realize that this was my new normal and I needed to change my response.

There are very few things that we can control but one thing we will always have the ability to control is ourselves and how we respond to things. Here I was at the age of twenty-seven and I was about to teach myself how to be responsible for my own emotions. It wasn't the baby's fault that she woke up in the middle of the night hungry and woke me up so that I could feed her. This is how life works. This was my life and it was time for me to learn how to change my perspective up a bit.

Coming from a lifestyle where I played the role of a mother to a grown woman who struggled with addiction, and then to being the mother of a little innocent baby, was hard. There is no other word for it other than difficult. This would require a total rewiring of my brain, seriously. This was something that I refused to give up on because it was very important to me that I become the absolute best mother that I can be for my child.

Up until this point in my life I had struggled with some anger, most specifically in moments that I felt disrespected and unheard. For thirteen years I, "Parented" my mom. I had thirteen years worth of becoming aggravated when she wouldn't just lie down and go to bed. I would go back to her room after just watching her put out a cigarette and she would have done lit another one. Well you know what can happen if someone falls asleep with a cigarette. Your house could catch on fire. I'd finally get her all situated and laying down and I would go get comfy in the bed drifting off to sleep, and ten minutes later I would hear her rummaging in the pantry. Well, what if she choked while she was eating? So then of course I would attempt to make her lie down and tell her she could eat tomorrow but another part of me didn't want her to go to bed hungry and felt bad so I'd stay awake with her until she was done thirty minutes later. Yes it took her this long to eat something if she was under the influence because she would constantly doze off while eating it. There is no other word for this lifestyle except emotionally draining.

If you aren't very familiar with or haven't ever experienced someone under the influence of pills, it can be comparable to someone who has had quite a bit of alcohol to drink. Experiencing this as a constant and unpredictable thing in my life was extremely frustrating. I never had any type of control of my own life. Well, the bigger picture showed that I actually did, but because she was my mom and I was her only child, I felt completely responsible for her and anything her actions while she was under the influence may cause.

Becoming responsible for an adult at the age of thirteen is something most children will never have to experience. This time in a child's life is so crucial for their adulthood. They are trying to figure out who they are and where they belong. They are basically hoping and praying that the world accepts them and if for one tiny reason they don't feel like it does, they change something up in an attempt to be accepted.

I honestly don't clearly remember how I felt at that age and I don't necessarily remember being hateful or mean to anyone, but if you ask any of my long time friends about who I was back then, they're best description would probably be intimidating. There is probably other words they would chose to use to describe me as well but they aren't appropriate or necessary to use. I'm not quite sure what may have prompted me to behave this way or act like I was better than anyone but I can guarantee that it's something I'm not proud of. I am sure there were bitter feelings and I'm sure I experienced some jealousy and envy because of all of the other girls my age that didn't have to experience what I was. Also, dealing with an addict doesn't exactly bring a mind to a state of happiness or joy. At least it didn't for me as a teenager.

So, with this being my normal for years, it unconsciously developed a constant negative state of mind for me. My brain developed habits like its first thought was the worst case scenario. It always immediately took offense to everything and always ended up being the victim on everything. It's a selfish way to look at things but it's really hard for us to understand that other people's feelings exist too and it's not all about us. Actually most of the time, it's never about us. Nine times out of ten, the situation or the people involved aren't even thinking about you or your feelings. They are thinking about their own. But I was a mom now. I was going to be raising a child in this big world and she needed me to be different. I could no longer harbor this child like way of thinking or the actions the childlike state of mind provoked. So again, I'll repeat, there are very few things we can control in this world but one thing we will always have the ability to control is ourselves and how we respond to things. I couldn't cling to my childhood and the, negative things that happened in it or to me. That's the beautiful thing about our lives; we have a choice to change it at any time. I could no longer excuse my childish behavior because of what all I had been through and encountered in the past. If anything has the power to change you, it's your child. And change was just beyond the horizon.

8

He Answers Prayers

I'm not sure if you have ever attempted to change anything about yourself but let me be the first to tell you that doing it alone, is pretty much impossible. For me it was anyway. I started January 1st, 2016 off with a daily devotional book that I had in my possession for years. I had gotten years prior as a Christmas gift and just put it to the side and forgot about it. God had a way of working like that. It literally turned up so random that it blew my mind that I had it all those years and never even opened it to see what it was. Shows you where I was in my spiritual life at that point. Toward the end of December I had found it and decided I would start reading it every day. I am that note taker in class that basically rewrites the book because my notes are very thorough. I never really did completely adopt the skill of true note taking because everything seemed important. There's no doubt I over did it but that's neither here nor there.

For each one of the days, the devotional provided two or three Bible verses. I would pick my favorite one and write it down for that day. That may have only lasted for about six months and then I just stopped doing it that way. I realized that I never went back and looked at them so it probably wasn't as useful for me as I initially thought it was. To this day, I do still read each day's devotional and look each Bible verse up simply because it plants the seed for the day; however I no longer write out my favorite verse. Each year I just start back on January first. Sometimes I wonder how different my life would have been if I had opened it up the day I received it as a gift and started using it then, but then I remember how perfect God's timing is and realize that I was meant to open it the day I did. It is so crazy how He perfects everything done at the hands of Him. I try not to question it because that interferes with faith.

This was a great start to my prayer of doing better, being better, and strengthening my faith. The more I would try to change about myself in order to be a better mom, the more I found myself relying on God. It was so crazy to me because everything I wanted to change or work on, no matter what I did, I felt like it could not be done by me alone. It all made sense though because if I could have done it on my own, I would have done it sooner.

It is so common for people to come to God with prayers when they really want something for themselves. They pray for things to go their way. These prayers look like, "God please let me get this job." or "God please let them accept my offer on this house." My prayers looked like, "God please let her sleep through the night." or "God please let her not be fussy this evening." Y'all, I really am not a fan of delivering news that you don't want to hear, but with this information, I am going to do just that. All of the prayers I've given as an example are self seeking prayers. God doesn't answer the prayers we have that we pray to Him in our favor. We have to give up the self seeking prayers because our only prayer through anything that He's listening for is that His will be done.

Talk about a game changer. I can't even imagine how many prayers I've prayed in my life that was prayers for me. In high-school, "Please let me get into classes with my friends." When I was pregnant, "Please let this sweet baby be a boy." When I was running late to work, "Please let all of the traffic lights be green and please let there be no traffic at 6:50 a.m. going through this school zone." Let's be real. That last one isn't even possible going through a school zone located in a middle school and high school area. We pray prayers like these and then get mad at God when He doesn't put us in the class with our friends. Our high hopes are let down when we find out we are having a different gender than we wanted. We come into work storming mad because God didn't make all of those lights green on our way in. This isn't how prayer works. We have to change our prayers. When we change our prayers we change our hearts. When we change our hearts, we change our perspective.

When I realized how upset I would get because God wasn't answering my prayers in my favor, it dawned on me. He's not going to make my life perfect in my eyes like I keep praying for Him to do. He is going to provide me with exactly what He knows I need in order to fulfill His plan for my life.

At this point, I started changing my prayers up. I started praying for patience in those moments that Laney couldn't tell me what was wrong and wouldn't quit crying. I started praying to have the ability to be more conscience of the things I was praying for in the exact moments that my struggle moments would arise. For quite some time it felt like the more I prayed about my weak spots, the more the situations that would trigger them would show up. If I can imagine, God was probably watching me thinking, "Let me see if she's able to realize this time that I'm trying to change her like she's been asking me to help her do." Meanwhile I'm thinking, "Are you serious right now? How come the things that I struggle with the most are showing up even more now that I've been praying harder about them?" It took me quite a bit of time to realize what God was doing. These were training sessions.

In the beginning, I felt like such a big failure through these training sessions because every single time, I would react and respond in the ways that I was trying so hard to change. I learned quite a bit about perseverance through this part of my life because over time, slowly but surely, I was starting to notice a difference. When we want something bad enough, we work as hard as we can to acquire it. I wanted Laney to have a mom like I had when I was little, a patient one.

I stayed pretty dedicated to becoming this mother who I had envisioned that I wanted to be. Some days are harder than others but if you have an idea of the things you want to be better at and do better at to be an example for your children, you stay dedicated. If you slip up, you just try harder the next time. I've learned that grace and realizing you have it is important to have for yourself. God gifts us with grace freely so we might as well remember that we are loved even through the moments we feel like we've failed and get up and try again.

In the meantime I had read a couple books to help with my parenting techniques. I just wanted to be sure I was doing things the best I could that would be beneficial to Laney in the long run. Anytime I felt like I was being faced with a new type of situation that involved her rather it be her not listening or telling me no over and over again, I researched how to handle it. I couldn't remember how mom handled me at these moments. As Laney gets older, I'll be able to be more like my mom was for me and reference memories when I need her for them because she was pretty amazing during my childhood and I remember so much. Prior to elementary school though, I am pretty unsure of quite a bit of what it takes in a mom to raise a baby.

My dad was pretty resourceful when I would question him about stuff. I didn't spend as much time with him as a child because my mom had full custody of me and he had full custody of my half brother, Skyler. Skyler is two and a half years younger than me and a lot of the time I would go spend weekends with my dad, Skyler would be spending those weekends with his mom. We were both on an every other weekend routine. I would go spend every other weekend with my dad and he would go spend every other weekend with his mom.

I didn't spend enough time with my dad to really get to feel him and his personality out. It was like I would get with him on Friday evening and then head home on Sunday evenings. Forty-eight hours every other weekend just wasn't enough to really develop a true relationship like I had developed with my mom. One thing always stood apparent about my dad in my mind and that was that he was a hero and he had a heart full of Jesus and that never wavered. Not even in the midst of chaos.

My dad had faced a few challenges along the way. Right around the age of thirty, he collapsed on the concrete floor of the airplane hangar that he was employed at as a mechanic, at and started having a seizure. They rushed him to the hospital and after a lot of testing they had found a brain tumor. After quite a bit of radiation he was able to recover and become cancer free.

A few years later, I was at that age that going out to my dad's where I was woken up on Sunday mornings for church was something I felt like was for the birds. I was at an age where they basically let me chose rather or not I wanted to go out there every other weekend. Well, I was growing up and all the things that were at one point in my life so much fun, were not necessarily as enjoyable as they once were. Plus, let's be honest. I had more freedom and fewer rules at moms and at the age of thirteen and fourteen, so as a newfound teenager, was this even something to debate about?

At one point my mom had told me that I better start going to spend more time with my dad. She said, "Your dad had those health issues and Kristen Jo you just never know what could happen." Man those words burned into my brain. They really hit home for me especially when within that next month we got a phone call stating that dad wanted to come pick me up so that we could talk. I think he had already told mom what was going on but she didn't tell me and she left it for him to tell me.

At that age I always remember dad driving smaller box looking cars. If you can remember the shape of cars in the early to mid nineties, you will know exactly what I'm referring to. One very vivid memory of my childhood about my dad was exactly that, his cars. He was over six foot tall so it always humored me to say the least.

This specific night that he came to pick me up, he picked me up at the fair. It was the weekend the fair was in town down at what used to be the fairgrounds that they have now made into a marina area. Talk about heartache. I don't own a boat though and never have so I won't knock the idea of taking away a place that housed quite a few of my fondest childhood memories. I used to cheer for a pee wee football team down there every Saturday. I used to attend the rodeo and the fair when it would come to town. Most definitely a place I will never forget.

I stood outside of the fenced area right at the front entrance and waited for dad to come. We had decided on a time for me to be waiting for him and right on time, he showed up. I hoped in the car and we drove away. I was at a point in my life where things didn't seem maybe as serious as they are for me today. I would have maybe appreciated the news more and understood what was going on better today, than I did at the age of thirteen. Dad told me that they had found an aneurism located in his brain on his most recent scan and that they were going to be doing some procedures. He assured me that everything would be okay and that he was fine but that he just wanted me to know what was going on.

I don't really remember many more details than that. I know they had to do surgery and go in and operate on that particular spot but other than that, I wasn't sure of what type of procedure or operation they would be doing. All I mainly remember him telling me about it was that he was going to be okay so I trusted him, and he was exactly right. Before I knew it, he had recovered and he had this cool scar that existed on his forehead right at his hairline. If he had a recent haircut, you could see it. Most people probably acknowledged it as just a normal scar. To me, it was a gentle reminder of the super hero he was.

I've always had this soft spot in my heart for my dad. He is such a gentle man and has been for as far back as I could remember. After my mom passed away, we both attempted to establish that bond that existed during my childhood. He would text me every Thursday evening to inquire about my week with a reminder that it was almost the weekend. At one point it had become a competition as to who could text who first. It was the sweetest.

Now that Laney was here, it was like he was getting to experience me all over again at that age. He said that she reminds him so much of me when I was little. He gave her a slightly different nickname than what he had given me as a child. He always called me spaghetti legs because I was so tiny. He assigned Laney the nickname of crazy legs. Her legs were nonstop as a baby if she was lying down and honestly that hasn't changed a bit now that she can walk.

9

A Greater Good In Everything

Right about the time that Laney was eighteen months, my dad started experiencing some minor medical issues. There would be moments that he would basically space out. What it seemed like was the start of this was when he wrecked his truck into the back of another vehicle at a stop light. I remember him seeming kind of confused when I asked him about what happened. There were other rather odd things that started happening as well. For instance, on a normal day it took dad about thirty minutes to get to work but one day it took him a little over an hour. When he walked in and realized he was actually late and that he had left the house at a normal time, confusion set in. He had no idea what he had done that made him take an extra thirty minutes getting to work.

He had experienced another episode shortly after that on his lunch break. My step mom called me while I was at work and had asked me if I would go get him because he had run off the road. He had no idea where he was and all that he could tell her was that he was on the bypass somewhere. Apparently some days when he would take lunch, he would take the scenic route to do his errands. At the end of this road that he was on there was one specific spot in the road that is quite a bit of a bend right before you get to the stop sign. For some reason, dad never turned the wheel on that turn and ran right into the ditch which kind of went down into an embankment.

I remember on the way to pick him up, complete panic had sat in. I started experiencing all of these uncomfortable feelings that I experienced when I would have to care for mom when she was under the influence. Dad wasn't by any means under the influence but the same fear of the unknown set in. It was a feeling I knew all too well and hadn't experienced in a long time and it felt the exact same as it used to. Not to mention my heart was breaking for my poor daddy. What in the world is going on, God bless him?

In the meantime as he is continuing to experience these random blur moments, he is heading in and out of doctor appointments to try and get to the bottom of what is going on. Of course the very first place they sent him was to his neurologist because of his history. They did all types of brain scans and they never turned up anything. There was no sign that there was anything in his brain that could be causing these episodes.

Besides having these episodes that would continue to happen unexpectedly, he started to experience some swelling in his eyes. At one point his eye lids had become so swollen that one of his eyes couldn't even open. It was one of the most heartbreaking things I have ever witnessed in my life. Dad never complained about it though. He kept showing up to work and he kept going in and out of doctor appointments. After the swelling of his eyes, his doctor sent him to an allergy specialist thinking that this could be something related to allergies. It was like we were turning in circles in search for answers and everywhere we turned, we came up with nothing.

Finally, they told dad to just go to the emergency room at a specific hospital in Nashville. The doctor had sent over numerous tests for them to run. I remember waiting impatiently for a phone call for answers as to what may have been going on. On this particular evening Ryan had to run to a hardware store right up the road about five minutes from our house. This hardware store is located right next to the grocery store that I sat in the parking lot of when I received the phone call of the tragic news of my mother's death.

Laney and I were sitting out in the parking lot while Ryan ran in the store and my step mother called to let me know what was going on. She specifically told me that they had found a spot that they were going to run some tests on located in my dad's lung and that his lymph nodes appeared to be swollen so they were also going to look into that as well. My heart sank as soon as I heard her say they found a spot on his lung. I was unsure of what exactly a lymph node was at this point and also unsure exactly what it did for the human body. I did the best I could to keep from sounding panicked or upset and told her to please let me know when they heard back from the doctor after further investigation of their initial find. I have to be honest, as soon as we hung up the phone; I typed, "Swollen lymph node" into a search engine and what immediately popped up as what could be a cause of swollen lymph nodes confirmed my initial thought of what this could be.

In the midst of everything, Ryan had recently gotten back into the truck. The more I read on swollen lymph nodes, the more tears rolled down my cheeks. It wasn't necessarily the fact that his lymph nodes were swollen that was prompting all of the things going through my head. It was because they found the spot on his lung, with also having the swollen lymph nodes, that was causing the panic that had taken over my heart and mind. At this point, there was so much to process and there was even more that was still unknown. I remember I kept trying to maintain my composure in front of Laney. Inside I was falling apart but on the outside I was doing the very best I could to hold it together.

Ryan kept trying to tell me all of the other things that it could be other than what my mind kept telling me it was. He was like, "Babe you have no idea what it could be. It could be anything. Just wait until all of the tests come back and it calls for all of this as a reaction, and then react to it. For now though, just breathe and get off of the internet." He was right. I shed a few more tears and then just kind of went numb for the rest of the evening. No matter what ever happens in our lives, if we are moms, motherhood is full time. We can't set it to the side. We can't pause it until we feel like doing it. We can't ignore it until it's convenient for us. It's full time and this particular night, it was needed extra. She helped keep me busy enough to keep my mind off of the news we were waiting for. There is no doubt in my mind that God knew that I would need Laney at this point in my life. She is my biggest proof of the perfection of His amazing timing.

That next morning, November 16th 2016, I got up and got ready as usual and stuck to my normal routine. Routine keeps me grounded. Routine is what I long for the most in the midst of chaos. I dropped Laney off at her daycare and headed to Nashville. They had kept dad over night so that they could run a biopsy on the place they had found and monitored everything that he had been experiencing. My step mom had gone back to Clarksville in the meantime to shower and to get some clothes in case they had to stay another night. Dad was still a little out of it from them having to sedate him in order to do his biopsy. The muscle specialist had come into dad's room while I was there and asked him if she could update me on everything that was going on. He agreed and she took me out in the hallway.

The news she gave me left me feeling like I needed someone to come pick me up off of the floor. She explained that until this last test that she was waiting on came back, she couldn't confirm what she suspected, but judging by her history in her career and what all she had seen over the years, this was what she thought it was. This is what I thought it was. It was cancer.

I walked back into his hospital room and just looking at his precious face with a smile that seemed as if it was permanent all of his life, made me want to burst into tears. It made my heart ache knowing that this man had already been through so much in his life and now he had to face this battle. I will never forget the words that came from his mouth when I walked back in to him with that smile. He said, "I'm going to beat it. I've beat it before. I'll beat it again."

Do you know what my dad did when he was delivered this news? He looked at the doctor and said, "I know it's got to be a tough job delivering news like this to people." He then proceeded to get up out of his hospital bed and stood and gave her a hug. There was something that my dad took with him everywhere he went, including into that hospital room where they presented him with the worst news of his entire life and that something was Jesus. When your heart is filled with Jesus like my dad's was, it can't be hidden.

This cancer was terminal. It was stage four of a very aggressive lung cancer and it had metastasized which meant it had spread to other parts of the body. His life could be prolonged with treatments of chemotherapy but with anything in life, the future is unpredictable. We weren't sure how long the chemotherapy would be beneficial to his body and would help slow the process of the cancer spreading. As you can imagine, fear came over me immediately.

I'm not sure what may come to your mind when someone says the word chemotherapy but when I was told they would start it on my dad in just a few weeks, my goal was to cook and provide him with the as many of the best meals that I could. I've always thought that chemotherapy makes people really sick to the point that they can't even hardly eat or keep food down. I remember looking at the calendar and in my head meal prepping and getting a count on all of the really good meals I could make before his first treatment.

I didn't want to smother him but deep down inside, I wanted to show up at his house every day and just be with him. I had such a difficult battle going on within me about all of this. I couldn't let on to anyone else what my mind kept telling me. My mind kept telling me to treat this as if cancer was going to take his life. I couldn't dare share these thoughts with anyone because of how negative they felt. I kept shaming myself for thinking this way. Then I would feel bad because I felt like I was disappointing God by feeling this way and even listening to what my mind was trying to convince me of. Since then though, I have learned that we simply can't disappoint God. My faith kept telling me that God is capable of performing miracles and that He could heal my dad. What research studies had shown about this type of cancer in this particular stage made it difficult for me to believe that my dad would overcome this unless it was God's will for him to continue to be here. This very experience showed me exactly what it looked like to trust God's will.

I felt like my heart was being forced to decide rather I was going to believe the facts that had been revealed in the past about this type of cancer or I was going to believe in God's miracles. Something in my mind had me convinced that I had to choose one. In this season of my life, I realized that both could exist together. Deep down I continuously prayed for a miracle. I also came to understand that if dad's time on earth was coming to an end because that was part of God's will it was something I needed to learn to trust.

10

The World Is In His Hands

There was so much to process at this point. Something that really tugged at my heart during this time was the bond that was being created between my dad and my daughter. It was already such an emotional thing for me to know that Laney would never know my mom but would she even get to have memories with my dad that she would be able to remember? It seriously felt like that the first Sunday we spent with dad at church after he was delivered the news of what he was facing, Laney came in with a magnet that automatically attracted her to dad.

You can't fathom this experience from my perspective. My soon to be two year old was establishing such a strong connection with my only surviving parent here to experience her and now I was faced with the possibility of this special bond being stripped away by cancer. Here we were at the holidays and I am going into them attempting to cherish every single second of them because this could be the last one I ever spend with my dad. My birthday is on Christmas so would my twenty-ninth birthday be the last one I celebrated with a parent here? Would I celebrate a thirtieth birthday without parents? Laney's birthday is New Years Eve so would the last birthday my dad ever celebrated with her be her second birthday?

There is nothing of this world that can comfort someone in a time such as this one. There is nothing of this world that can soothe the aching pain that a heart feels when it is faced with something so life altering. There is nothing of this world that can provide you with answers to all of the questions that surface when you experience so much unknown at one time. There is nothing of this world that can direct you when you have no idea what to do with the emotions that are provoked from so many different feelings at one time. What I needed and what my heart desired in such a devastating time already existed in my heart and had been there since the day I was made. It was God.

This was the point in my life that I realized that no one on earth would ever completely understand me or what my heart feels. I realized that I should no longer expect someone to be able to give me the things I had unconsciously wanted from them. This was when I realized that no matter how much explaining I do and no matter how much I expressed my sadness and sorrow to other people, they would never understand and they weren't supposed to. God wired us this way. This was when God showed me that anything I could ever need or want for the rest of my life, no matter what it was, could always be found in Him which always existed in me. When I truly felt this, I knew that this next chapter of my life was going to require more Him and less me.

Laney and I started going to church with my dad and step mom every Sunday. Dad played the drums in the band they had there at the church which Laney seemed to think was pretty awesome. It blew her mind to see papa up there. She always danced to the music that the band played during worship. It was such an uplifting place to be at a time in our lives that had tendencies to want to drag us down.

I was so proud of Laney for how she acted while we were there. I kept her in the congregation with us and she did anything from color in coloring books to putting stickers from the tip of my dad's fingertips all the way up to his elbows. We would put all of those stickers back on the sticker sheet that they had come from at the end of the church service. The next Sunday we would come and do the same thing again. We would do this until there was no stick left on the sticker and start on a new sheet. Laney had no idea what this meant for us as adults, less money on stickers.

They scheduled dad's chemotherapy sessions on Wednesday, Thursday, and Friday and they would be every other week. I volunteered to take him Thursdays, so every Thursday I would go pick him up and take him to his appointments. This time was special for us because we didn't get any one on one time together other than the thirty minutes driving him to the chemotherapy clinic and the thirty minutes driving him home from there. It was a ritual for us to swing through Burger King's drive thru and get dad a double cheeseburger. He couldn't stand it but I wouldn't ever let him pay. He would try to give me the money every time but I refused. I knew it was important for me to do what I could for him no matter how big or small it was.

Every chemotherapy appointment I would pull up at his house and he would come out cigarette in hand and ready to be lit for the ride. I didn't ever let people ever smoke in my car but when he asked if he could, I told him he could. If he enjoyed riding in the passenger seat smoking a cigarette, well then light it up. Smoking was one of the first things he mentioned after he had gotten diagnosed. He held one of the cigarettes up and said, "I'm not giving these up; I'm going to smoke these until the day I die." He would usually get in two cigarettes on the way there and two on the way back home. His chemotherapy drip bag took exactly one hour to drip. It was in the exact some type of bag that they put saline in when they hook you up to an IV at a hospital. When I saw that, it blew me away. I didn't realize that medical technology had come this far. They would just access his port that was located in his chest and allow all of the fluid in the bag to go into his body over the course of an hour.

The staff at the clinic was amazing. It takes special people to work at a place like this because of the type of situations some people are in when they come here. They always treated dad so well and catered to anything he needed. Because of the chemo liquid that was pumped into his body during this process, it would cause him to get cold so here they also provided a pillow and a blanket. Dad went through every session reclined in that chair with a pillow under his head and a blanket to keep him cozy. For dad, chemo sessions meant a guaranteed nap time. For me, chemo sessions meant watching him sleep.

The way that it was explained to me is basically that they would continue these chemo treatments until they no longer seemed to be beneficial to him. What this meant, was that as long as his scans showed that nothing was growing or getting progressively worse, he would continue chemotherapy treatments. He did these up until April of 2017. At this point they would give his body a break because he had received so much. A lot of people don't realize that while chemotherapy does tend to fight the cancer cells to some extent and keep it from progressing as quickly, it also kills off the good cells as well in the process.

By June, dad would start experiencing some confusion and had experienced some random seizures as well during the course of chemotherapy. God bless him that whole last six months he stayed pretty banged up from falls. How could something be so cruel to someone so amazing? It just didn't seem fair to see someone so special have to experience so many challenges.

On June 18th, Laney and I attended church with dad and got to witness him play the drums for the last time. He seemed so confused this particular day and he struggled to figure out what he was supposed to do next when everyone in the band exited from the stage. Dad just sat there and looked so helpless. His balance wasn't at full potential so when he did finally stand up, he swayed. From my seat I had wished I could just pick him up and bring him back to his chair without anyone noticing. I just wanted to hold him and tell him everything was going to be okay. Meanwhile, I felt like I needed someone to do just that for me. This was the last time dad would ever attend church and what made it incredibly special was that it was Father's Day.

He and my step mom came over that evening and we all sat around and enjoyed each other. I sat beside my dad on the couch and I remember at one point I tilted my head over so that it was snuggled into his chest and I just embraced what I knew at the time was a very special moment. I can specifically remember thinking to myself, "Remember this night. Be here. Be here right now. Be present." Throughout this chapter of my life I had so many pep talks where I would have to bring myself back to the moment and truly live in it. In society today, it's really hard to do that because of what the world has come to. I had to train myself to do it though. I knew these times were incredibly special.

There's a whole new part of you that surfaces when you are told that someone you dearly love has had a timer put on their life. Because I had lost my mom I knew that one thing was very important and that was pictures. My mom didn't like taking pictures at all so she had very few of them. What was really heartbreaking was that she and I had so few together. I didn't want to bombard dad with constantly taking pictures because then that's just awkward. So I had gotten pretty good at snapping them in special moments, most of which he probably had no idea about. I had to be sneaky to make it less awkward. Thankfully though, I knew the worth of a photo and knew how special they are when that's all you have left of someone. Again, how do you share with someone that you are taking countless pictures because of this reason during a time like this?

So this evening, it took all I had to ask for a picture. I asked that a picture be taken with Dad, Skyler, and I. Thank God I did because it was the last one we have together. It was the last picture I ever took with my dad, on the last Father's day I ever spent with him. Talk about a cherished photo. Dad had aged so much, even in that last seven months. I didn't realize how powerful cancer was until I looked at that picture.

That following Saturday, my step mom called and asked if Ryan could come and help her get dad up off the floor. He had fallen and couldn't get up. I'm sure Ryan had kept the majority of the detail from me to protect me but he told me that when he was trying to tell dad to stand in an attempt to help with the process of getting him up, he just looked at him puzzled. He said it was like his brain wasn't able to communicate with his legs in order to prompt them to move. My step mom took him to the hospital that day and scans confirmed that the cancer had spread to his brain. Once cancer gets to a person's brain and it's as aggressive as dad's cancer was, it moves quickly.

11

God Is Always With Us

Dad didn't necessarily realize or see the things that we were able to see. If he had done something that wasn't normal, he wasn't able to realize himself that it wasn't normal. It was obvious that the cancer was present in his nervous system. The things that had made him independent were slowly fading away. Something as simple as getting up from a chair became dangerous. It was like his mind told him to do it but his legs never got the message. It was such a painful thing to witness.

He was admitted into the hospital in Nashville the day after we had confirmation that it had spread to his brain. He was by far, safest here and most certainly well taken care of by the hospital staff. Laney's childcare center is located on a highway that goes from Clarksville to Nashville, so on the days I would visit dad, I would leave straight from her daycare and go to the hospital. I like to call that route the scenic route. It felt more soothing than the interstate.

In order to change, we have to get out of our comfort zone. God was on the move in my life at this point and He made it obvious. Time after time I would be forced to overcome little things that no one probably even realized was a struggle for me in this season of my life. God knew my struggle though and He was always there to comfort me.

Remember when I mentioned that mom would pick me up and take me to doctor appointments even after I moved out? Also, do you remember that unforgettable moment that I experienced with my dad when I was in labor and he softly kissed me on my forehead? I needed this right now. I needed that type of comfort in my life. While Ryan was as loving and understanding as he could possibly be for me during this time and all of my friends were as caring and as compassionate as I had ever witnessed in our friendships, they weren't my parents. It wasn't their duty to comfort me in the same way that my parents could. The kind of comfort that my heart desired and that my soul longed for was one that could only be provided by a parent. It was the kind of comfort that no one on earth could provide for me at this time.

I reminded myself so much of my mom throughout all of this. My mom was so nurturing and it was like the moment she entered a hospital room, she became a full time nurse. She would wait on someone hand and foot if she was given the chance. I found a whole new appreciation of watching her be such a wonderful caretaker through this whole experience.

The first few days dad seemed to be doing okay and was remaining pretty independent when it came to eating. He would still cut up with someone if they opened the opportunity for it. That was one thing about my dad, he was hilarious. Skyler is just like him too so when you got the two of them together it was guaranteed that you would laugh until your abs ached and you could hardly breath. He had gotten pretty quiet though and had started using a phrase that anyone who witnessed it, will never forget. His response to basically anything said at this point was, "No doubt." I still use it to this day and any time I hear the word doubt, I think of my dad. He did sleep quite a bit but I knew that's what was best for him, rest. The time he did spend awake, you could bet he'd be smiling.

He spent about ten days here and about half way through his stay the hospital called in the middle of the night and suggested that we come to the hospital in preparation of what could be him passing. Throughout his stay out of these ten days he would have small seizures and they had told us that a stroke could be possible because of how quickly the cancer was spreading through his brain. With the cancer being so present in his nervous system, and all of the activity with it moving through his brain, it kept causing small seizures. This particular night though, they said that they believed he had a big seizure or that he had a stroke because they couldn't get him conscious. When we finally made it to the hospital he had woken up. We stayed there with him until he was comfortably resting and asleep and we all packed back in the car and went home to get some much needed rest.

He was on a waiting list for a rehabilitation center in Clarksville. They had drawn up all of the paperwork and sent in everything necessary to hopefully get him moved closer to home. This ten day hospital stay period felt like an entire month. Every day someone from Clarksville would drive down there and be with him. It would be me, my step mom, or my brother. It was working out that I would basically go every other day.

Every time I pulled out of Laney's childcare center to head that way, it was like somehow, automatically, I felt more connected to God. I relied on Him so much through all of this which plays such a huge part in my relationship with Him today. If you can imagine taking some of your biggest fears and combining them together and overcoming them at one time, that is what was happening in this.

There were a few things to take note of here. At this time in my life, I was extremely claustrophobic, I avoided elevators at all cost, parking garages freak me out, and the more distant I get from doors that reach the outside, the higher my anxiety gets. Well, guess what? I had to face them and overcome all of them every time I went to visit him. I would literally climb seven flights of steps every time I went to visit him by myself which was every time except maybe two. The other things couldn't be avoided. I had to park in the parking garage and his

106

room was on the seventh floor so I was nowhere near an, exit door. All of these things are obviously related and because I'm such a thinker, I have tried to reference things in my past that could have caused the reasoning to these things I really struggle with and always come up empty handed. Either way, all of these different situations that I was terrified of, were out of my control. They all made me uncomfortable but I was forced to do them. Every single time I prayed through these moments that in the past would send me into panic and my mind into complete chaos, I would experience so much peace.

It wasn't long before I realized that during this time I was starting to experience some of the same feelings of panic and nervousness that I would when my mom would be under the influence. It had been so long since I felt these that when they hit me, they hit me hard. I would go in to dad's hospital room knowing there was no way that I could prepare myself for today's visit because I wasn't sure of his condition. Every day seemed to be slightly harder than the next. You just don't know what to expect during something so unpredictable from one moment to the next. On the days I would help feed him his meal, I would be so nervous that he was going to choke. He coughed so much too. I would be afraid that he would get choked coughing too much. If he would even move in the least bit, I panicked. During this part of my life, as I faced all of these things that I was so fearful of, I realized that I feared them because I had no control of them. I realized that no matter how much I panicked or how much anxiety that I would allow them to cause to me, if it was going to happen, it would happen. This is when I learned to pray that no matter what may happen, that God just be with me.

Dad was moved to a rehabilitation center in Clarksville, about five minutes from my house and seven minutes from where I worked which no doubt in my mind was a God thing. I would go see him on my lunch breaks or after I got off from work. Some days it was both. You had to kind of limit yourself to visiting when it came to this point. I fought really hard with this part because I didn't want dad to be alone but there was also nothing that anyone could do at this point. It was so sad to just sit there. I remember my mom doing that when her mom was really sick with cancer and it really takes a toll on someone to ever experience this side of cancer much less spend every moment in it. I finally had to tell myself that dad would not want me to sit in that room for hours upon hours and cry.

By the time dad had gotten here, he had already pretty much lost his appetite and was hardly able to talk anymore. He was put in a room with two beds but he was the only one in there, thankfully. I can't imagine experiencing something like this with him sharing a room with someone we didn't know. Dad had a lot of visitors here so the extra space made a huge difference. He was loved by everyone who met him so this allowed for all of the visitors of the lives he touched.

The rehabilitation center put him on a liquid diet about two days after he had gotten there because he had gotten to the point that he just couldn't eat. Every time I walked into that room, my heart literally hurt. Cancer is an emotional roller coaster. I never knew how angry I could be at something that I had never seen that was running like a wildfire through my dad's body and slowly taking his life. You literally get to a point that you start praying for God to take your loved one and bring them home with Him so they don't have to suffer anymore.

There was a battle going on within me as to rather or not I should take Laney to see him. I knew that she would bring him joy but I also didn't want her seeing him like that to be scary for her. Up until this point, he had a picture of her that sat on his tray where the food usually goes and he stared at nothing more his entire hospital stay, than he did that picture of her. His face had become expressionless at this point and he couldn't smile anymore but you could see it in his eyes what it meant to him to have that picture next to him.

On the 4th of July, I decided to finally take her up there and I am so glad I did. It was the most bitter sweet moment I have ever experienced in my life. She kept telling us that papa was sleeping when he would close his eyes. I think if dad could have talked he probably would have thanked me. That was a moment I tried to truly live in. That was the last time my baby would ever get to be with one of my parents.

On July 6th I went to visit with him when I got off work. I walked in and there was a peace that I immediately felt that I had not felt on any other visit. Prior to today, every day I would be preparing to go visit with him, my nerves were so unsettled. It is hard to see anyone in the condition that the last stage of cancer causes. It is cruel. It seems inhumane. It's awful. In that room with him this particular day was nothing but peace. The room was filled with complete peace that is so unforgettable for me. I sat there with him and held his sweet hand. I didn't have that urge in me to leave like I did every day previously caused by fear of the unknown. I had complete peace. I even stayed longer than I normally did in the prior days. After spending about two hours there, I got up and kissed him on his forehead. I told him I loved him and it was the first time I had left him and felt so at peace.

12

Becoming Fearless

The very next day as I prepared to leave work to go see him, my step mom called me and said that he had passed away. My heart was so calm when those words came from her mouth because I knew he was fully at peace and was with Jesus. I knew that he wasn't lying in that hospital bed completely helpless listening to all of those who visited him and talked to him that he couldn't respond to. I knew that God had rescued him from that cruel battle with cancer, no doubt.

There's something that I will never forget about my dad's entire fight with cancer and that is that he never complained. He never made it look like or ever acted like he was losing a battle. He didn't complain the day that they diagnosed him with it. He didn't complain the day that he was hospitalized two weeks prior to his death. He never wasted one breath on complaining. If I could imagine what it looked like to have one hundred percent faith in Jesus, it looked exactly like my dad did in his battle with cancer. He knew that no matter how powerful cancer looked on the outside, God was the most powerful within his heart.

Behind the scenes I was trying to adjust to the idea and painful reality that both of my parents now resided with Jesus. This can be a really scary thing in the beginning and honestly, every time it crossed my mind, my heart sank. The best way I can describe it at the age of twenty-nine was that my hand had been let go of. Imagine a small child with a parent or guardian in the middle of the grocery store. The child is holding the adult's hand but for some reason it lets go and ends up wandering off. That child is going to feel very fearful. It is going to be looking around hoping to be found and rescued by someone that can help it. I almost felt stranded. It felt like something in me had ended and I can't even express necessarily what I mean by that. It is something that can only be understood once it is experienced. It is something that could only be accepted and become adjusted to with the help of God.

We ended up having a visitation for four hours on one evening and then a small visitation before the hour of the funeral service the following day. For anyone who was able to attend dad's funeral, I can assure you that dad's funeral was one of the best services they have ever attended. It is hard for me to write best and funeral in once sentence together but this is worthy of it. If someone had attended the funeral not ever meeting my dad or necessarily even knowing my dad prior to that service, I am confident the preacher left everyone there that day with a very impactful experience. It described exactly who my dad was and it was nothing short of amazing. If someone could leave this earth and it was possible for them to leave with a bang, my dad did through the remarkable words stated by the preacher that day. He will always be one of my most favorite preachers. He was always one of my dad's most favorite people.

The morning of my dad's funeral, as I was dropping Laney off at daycare, I got a call from my mom's older brother who I call Bub and he told me that papa was at the emergency room and that he had taken him there the evening before. Bub lived with papa at the time and had for years. As independent as papa was, he did let Bub help him with a few things so it was beneficial for papa to have him around, especially since papa was eighty-seven years old. Bub said that papa's appendix had ruptured and that they performed surgery but that after a few days, he would be on the road to recovery and back home before we knew it. I asked him if he needed me to come up there or needed me to bring anything to them and he said he didn't. I told him that I would come up to the hospital to visit him after dad's funeral was over and that I would see him then.

After dad's grave side service ended, I went to the hospital to visit with papa. He was in the critical care unit at the hospital in town and was in quite a bit of pain but seemed to be doing fine. He had his heart set on coming home within the next few days and told me to go on home that it wasn't necessary I stay for a long period of time because he was fine and everything was going to be okay.

Because papa's body was eighty-seven years old and he wasn't exactly in the best of shape, his body started struggling to fight off the infection that had spread to his body when his appendix ruptured. His body was having an extremely hard time healing from the surgery that was done to remove his appendix. Within about four days of being there, he was put on a ventilator to help with his breathing since his lungs were really having a hard time operating and was put into a medical induced coma in hopes that his body would attempt to heal while he was at a full state of rest.

He remained like this for about a week and the doctors were doing the best they could to explain the severity of it to my uncle who seemed to be struggling to understand. After lots of phone calls to papa's surviving siblings, numerous one on one conversation with the doctor, and reassurance to Bub from papa's siblings and me that he was doing the right thing, he had the doctor remove the ventilator. In a very short period of time on July 22nd, 2017, papa's heart stopped.

My entire life felt completely out of control the entire month of July 2017 as you can imagine. I was in shock at all the events that had taken place that month. One precise thing that I never doubted through it all though was God's plan. It was through this season of my life that I learned to trust Him more than ever. This was a wilderness season.

You see, one thing I've learned about God is that He never brings us to anything with any intention to harm us. He brings us to situations and moments that are meant to strengthen us. His intention behind everything in our lives is to help us grow. Those moments that we find ourselves in that we feel as if no one understands, those moments are meant for us to rely on Him. God was using this season of my life to change me and to change my heart. He does things like this in order to prep us for our next mission that He has for us to fulfill.

Bub and I went down to the funeral home to do the finishing touches to the arrangements. I say finishing touches because papa had written up his own obituary and paid for his funeral about twenty years prior when my grandmother passed away. His thought process paid off for this because I can't imagine how much cheaper it was twenty years prior than they are today and we all know cheap was his route. That's one thing that always blew my mind about him and that was how his mind operated. Every time I would visit him there were envelops spread about the kitchen table he always sat at with numbers added up on the back of them. There was never any indication on the envelopes as to exactly what he was adding but there's no doubt in my mind that it was always money. The man saved every penny he could and rarely spent a dime on anything. He was very frugal but equally intelligent. He was a simple man as well and never wanted or needed anything more than what he already had. If I had to guess, the suit that we buried him in was probably at least twenty years old.

His grave side service was done with full military honors. It blew my mind how perfectly everything flowed while the soldiers fulfilled their duties at the cemetery. There was a slight struggle with folding the flag they eventually presented us with. They couldn't get it to fold perfectly so they had to try quite a few times. It was the end of July so you can only imagine how much sweat was dripping off of these men's faces as they worked so hard to get this done perfectly. Each time they would get it done, it would then be presented to the highest ranking officer standing at the end of the casket and he would tell them to refold it. I personally am not much of a perfectionist at all. You should see me fold a set of sheets! So for me the tiny thing that seemed incorrect to the man in charge didn't bother me at all and it would have been the last thing that I was concerned with when they handed me the flag if they had handed it to me that way. I realized though it wasn't about that at all. On the surface it may have seemed that way but on a more in depth level it was about the type of perfection and professionalism that was involved in what it takes to create and to maintain the greatest and strongest military in the world. I've always said that my utmost respect goes to any soldier who has ever served our country and I mean that with every inch of me. This day though, I gained a whole new aspect of what it means to be a soldier dedicated to our country. It takes one hundred percent sacrifice rather it is serving in a war or serving a brother that served previously by standing in what feels like one hundred plus degree weather folding a flag numerous times until it is perfect.

Over the years I had always kept in contact with papa. He had been my only surviving grandparent for the past eleven years so I always tried to maintain the best relationship I could with him. I would usually try to call and talk to him once a week. Of course he was retired and really didn't get out and do too much so the conversation was always kind of limited. I think the fact that I called meant more to him than anything. It's always the little things that mean the most and over the years I've learned that a lot of people don't always mention how much something means to them and there's nothing at all wrong with that.

Out of all of my grandparents, he was the one I had the least of a relationship with. He wasn't the easiest to develop a close relationship with because there really wasn't a lot that we could relate to each other on. He was one of those tough old men that had seen some things back in his day. There were days I would go over there and bring him breakfast and sit at the table and listen to war story after war story. Some I had heard at least five times but I would always act just as surprised and blown away at the heroic effort it took for him to even survive some of the things he told me. I listened to them over and over again because it brought him joy to tell them.

Every year for Thanksgiving and Christmas he would tell me not to worry about cooking. I never worried, I just cooked. He was pretty independent and never wanted anything to be done for him. He was stubborn and seemed to only get more stubborn with each year that passed but that didn't change how much I loved him.

This man had been through numerous wars, painfully watched his wife die to cancer, buried his youngest son who had just turned thirty-three and buried his only daughter who was only fifty-two years old. I have to say the only time I saw him cry was the two times he was told that his children had passed. It wasn't even really a cry; it was just a few tears shed. He was as tough as they come but if I could see deep into his heart, I bet I'd be able to see a couple broken areas. He never let on at all that he was ever hurting or that anything ever bothered him because some people just don't express how they really feel that's why I always just chose to love him as hard as he'd let me love him. You can never go wrong with loving people.

Speaking of love, he sure did love his sweet Laney. Every time I would bring her over there to visit him, he would light up like a Christmas tree. He thought she was the neatest thing and always enjoyed teasing her. He would get the biggest kick out of her and laughed harder than I had ever heard him laugh. Her an I would show up with breakfast at least once every two weeks and he thought it was the funniest thing for her to scoop what was basically one whole packet of ketchup up onto one hash brown and eat it. He would set her up on his knee and they would laugh and carry on. It was one of the most precious things I've ever witnessed.

Laney sure did love both of her papas and watching how she interacted with them was so incredibly special to me. How in the world was I supposed tell a two and a half year old that both of her papas have passed away? Well, it's simple, you just do. As a parent, I just wanted to protect her from being hurt. I didn't want her to be sad that she would never get to see either of her papas again. My heart was aching because two people that brought so much joy to her life, that she had always had the best of time with, were no longer here to share those moments with her. How do you even explain death to a toddler? I can answer this simply; you tell them that they're with Jesus. This was a perfect time to introduce faith to Laney even if she didn't understand. Little did I know that we were both being introduced to it at the same time, on two completely different levels. I had always known it, but had never been truly introduced to what it could do for my soul. The Lord always works in mysterious ways like that. It was from the next season of my life that I discovered that joy can't be found in things.

13

Peaceful Pieces

Obviously, I had just experienced quite a bit of chaos and tragedy and honestly, I was a little uncertain how I would bounce back from July 2017. Remember how I stated that my mom lost her mom and her grandfather in the same year, twenty years prior? I was incredibly terrified of that ever happening to me because I lived through and witnessed the damage it could do to someone and how it had the capability to affect them. I specifically remember dropping to my knees in my living room floor and crying and just praying for God to give me the strength to carry me through such a huge life altering experience. I prayed so hard that He would just wrap His arms around me and lead me through.

On one of the days in one of those last weeks of my dad's life, complete panic came over me when I realize that dad's life was slowly coming to an end and I remember thinking to myself, "Oh my goodness, please don't let papa pass away this year too." This weighed on me and my heart so much during this time so you can only imagine where my mind went when Bub called me that morning and told me that papa was in the emergency room. It is amazing what our minds do when we allow it to run our life entirely. My mind was notorious for thinking the worst and had trained itself to do that over the past decade basically. But let me tell you about God, this world in its entirety runs on His time. My life went from being fearful of my father and grandfather passing away in the same year, to the reality of my father and grandfather passing away in the same month, two weeks apart.

When it's someone's time to go because that is God's plan for them, it's their time. God places each and every one of us here to fulfill what He has planned for our lives. When we have served in such a way that fulfills His purpose for our lives, He brings us back home with Him. We literally never know when God will need us or anyone in this world for that matter, back. This was confirmed in my life with this exact situation. God took one of my worst fears and showed me how I could overcome it with Him.

I have been a Christian my entire life, but I never necessarily knew how to walk with God or how to have a close relationship with Him. Becoming a mom and wanting to change things about myself that I felt so powerless in changing because I had been that way for years, gave me the eagerness to learn how to develop a relationship with Him and learn how to walk with Him with intention. Looking back, it pretty much blows my mind that shortly after my heart began to long for a closer relationship with God, I experienced so much that required Him to get me through it.

The first thing I had to do was come to terms with everything that had happened. It felt like my world was spinning for a solid month. I mean, I guess in a sense it was. Everything still operated as it usually did except for me. I had spent three days short of a month, in and out of hospitals and a rehabilitation center every single day. I longed to feel normal again and have my routine back.

I learned something about routine when it comes to dealing with death. Routine is one thing I desperately needed back after experiencing loss. I knew that if I were to seclude myself that depression could creep up on me quickly. We are most vulnerable when we set ourselves apart from what was our normal prior to our loved one passing away. After every loss I've experienced, I know I have probably blown some minds by showing back up to work the day after the funeral but for myself, it was so necessary. You are that broken hearted and that devastated that if you spend days and weeks home, dwelling, you will literally fall into depression.

Thankfully, God knew exactly what I needed to help get me through this so two and a half years prior, He had blessed me with a beautiful baby girl that is the light of my life. Through this season of my life He showed me that experiencing moments helped to heal a broken heart. This wasn't something that was always apparent to me though. It wasn't something magical that just dawned on me one day. There was a time shortly after their deaths that I would find myself annoyed and wanting to be left alone. It was like my flesh wanted to go in a corner and I wanted to separate myself from everything. I still showed up to work every day. I still put away dishes and did laundry. I still bathed my baby girl every day. There was a part of me though that kept saying, "Just leave me alone and let me grieve. Let me be sad about this. Let me have a pity party. Let me be in my feelings." But the more I tried to be there and experience all of this sadness and stay in it, the shorter my temper was and the angrier I felt. Then I remembered I had a daughter that was watching this and was able to pick up on all of it and that for me was not okay.

It was through this season of my life that God showed me that my relationship with Him was dependent on me. He showed me that this is not an easy relationship to maintain in such a fast paced world that is so advanced and full of distraction everywhere we turn. He showed me that He will always be there. Anytime I call upon Him you can bet He will be there, that's how He works. But like anything, if we want something bad enough, we do everything we can to achieve it and I was back to my main mission and that was being the best mom that I could be for my baby and that meant a full time relationship with God. That meant making God a priority.

In the midst of attempting to bounce back from July, I took on the task of sorting out my grandfather's estate. I figured out pretty quickly what all of those numbers were probably related to that were always written on the backs of envelopes that sat on his kitchen table. I spent phone call after phone call trying to sort out all of the bits and pieces of things I was finding. The man had two filing cabinets in his bedroom but apparently it was just for storage purposes with no filing method. God rest his soul, there's no doubt in my mind that his filing method remained very precise in his own head but to me, trying to sort it all out, required celebratory drinks in honor of him the day I closed those books.

This was kind of stressful for me because I'm not one to just hop in the driver's seat of something so big and confusing but I did and thankfully God had placed a special person in my life about a year prior that would help me every step of the way. This would be one of the many things he helped me with and I honestly try not to miss a day thanking God for him.

This special person was brought onto our team during a huge change at the company I work for. Shortly after he was hired on, he became my boss and most definitely one of my most favorite people in the world. It didn't take us long at all to connect. If there was a male version of me, he is it. I call him my mentor and by far, best one of all times hands down. He grew up in Clarksville so we know a lot of the same people and actually he and his wife both pretty much know my entire family. That's the main way God connects us all is through people. He shows us he exists here and walks among us through people he brings into our lives. God shows up big for me through my mentor and he probably has no idea how much I see God through him. That's what's so awesome about God. He resides in everyone but a lot of people don't even realize how much He radiates through them. But if you know God, you always see Him in others.

It is pretty cool because he's about the same age as my parents and went to school with some of their siblings. Now that both of my parents have gone to be with Jesus, I turn to him for those moments I need wisdom and let me tell you, he's full of it. It's so crazy how God places people in our lives that we don't even know we need, but He does it and for that I'm thankful. He was exactly who I needed to be added to my story and crazy enough I fit right into his. This was nothing short of a God thing for sure.

During all of this change that was very obvious to the rest of the world on the outside, what was changing on the inside was happening so beautifully. Through all of the chaos, I had found that what fulfilled me the most were the moments that I was fully present in. Those moments could range anywhere from watching a sunset or coloring with my daughter.

One specific sunset that I remember being the most peaceful was the one I witnessed on July 2, 2017. I had gone to visit my dad that day in the hospital and that whole visit he never spoke a word because he couldn't talk anymore. His cancer had gotten so bad that he couldn't use his voice. This shattered my heart completely and it was the harsh reality of what was happening. When I left the hospital that day, I left there not knowing how to find comfort in the midst of such devastation.

I had a feeling come over me that at the time I didn't realize was God and all of a sudden I had a very strong urge to get to a place to watch the sun set that evening. Without even a second thought after that, I drove straight to my dad's church parking lot. I remember sitting there and feeling so peaceful that evening. Something in that sunset told me that everything was going to be okay. My heart had finally felt a sense of calm for the first time in a long time. That sunset and being in that church parking lot to experience it brought me to a state of peace. It was a moment I will never forget.

Since that day, I've chased many sunsets. The house I resided in at the time had a huge line of trees right across the street from it. Our back yard was filled with trees and we had neighbors behind us. We were living right in the middle of town which made it very convenient because everything we needed was right down the road. Because of the lack of the view I had there in seeing the sun set, I would get in my car and drive around in panic in an attempt to find the perfect spot to actually see it set. I may or may not have broken a few laws in an attempt to get to my viewing spot rather it be speeding or rolling through a stop sign. For you, a sunset may not be worth a two-hundred dollar speeding ticket but for me it was, depending on how much my heart longed for comfort that day. I'm sure it looks crazy to other people, but I've learned that sometimes it will look that way to others in our own pursuit of a relationship with Jesus and that's okay with me.

14

No Timing More Perfect

In August Ryan and I discussed maybe moving to a house that had a little more space because we were busting at the seams in that one. Ryan and I listed our home and got it set up with our real estate agent to be emailed any time something new came up in our desired area. We wanted to go back to the side of town that we grew up on. When we bought our first home, the home value was cheaper in the area we settled for which was right in the middle of town, than it was back where my roots were planted in a little area called Sango.

There was a house that I fell in love with that was right in our price range but when we went to look at it, it had some water issues in the basement. The house was being sold as is so it was something that would probably take some major money to first fix the problem and then fix all of the damage the problem had caused. I couldn't get my mind off of the floor plan of the home. It was to the point that Ryan contacted a friend that was a builder and I called our agent and asked if we could find a piece of land to build that same floor plan on. Well, there are a lot of legalities and politics to all of that so that was not an option for us. Looking back if I could have seen what God was up to it would have been very obvious that these roadblocks for what I wanted were being put up for a reason. He's pretty good about protecting us in such a way that we don't get what we want because He knows what's best for our lives. He sees the bigger picture and that wasn't His plan for me and my family.

Obviously our realtor knew how much I loved that floor plan because I couldn't stop talking about it. It had the perfect size kitchen and a huge, spacious dining room. All of the bedrooms were up stairs and were a pretty decent size. It had the sweetest front porch. Two must haves for me on the house we were buying were that it had to have a big kitchen and a big front porch. The must have for my husband was that it either had to already have a shop for him to run his business out of or have enough room for a shop to be built on. We weren't having much luck.

After about two or three weeks of looking around and a couple of people interested in ours, our agent said she had found a foreclosure house what was kind of laid out like the one I couldn't get my mind off of, but that it wasn't in the area that we were wanting. It just so happened that Ryan was already out that way mowing some client's property so he drove by there to look at it. He stated that it would at least be worth it to have our agent meet us out there so that we could look at it.

Of course I had so many mixed feelings about this because that's not where I wanted to be. I was unfamiliar with that side of town and I was not at all one to step out of my comfort zone when it came to big decisions like this. It was on the complete opposite side of town that I wanted. So I pretty much had to pep talk and do a lot of convincing to myself to at least just give it a chance and go look at it so we scheduled a time to meet our agent out there.

We pulled up to this house which was about a ten minute drive from town, out in the country. That part of it was kind of sweet because growing up, my dad's parents house was about that far from town so it triggered little memories of my childhood. Their country side was on a different side of town though. This side of town, out in the country, I was very unfamiliar with which was why I was so hesitant to even go look at this one. Ryan and I got out of the truck and I walked around the back of the house into the back yard and it literally took my breath away. This was home.

That sunset that I had chased for months could be found just by standing in this back yard. There was a farm located in front of it with no neighbors across the street. There was a farm located behind it with our back yard neighbor being fields away. This beauty sat on a one acre piece of property with enough room to build a shop for Ryan's business, a kitchen big enough to host any type of gathering I had ever dreamed of, and a front porch big enough to accommodate a few rocking chairs. This was it! I wanted it! Ryan and I both immediately fell in love.

Because it was a foreclosure we would need a few things related to the buying and selling process to happen perfectly. With a normal home buying process, you can get a contract that states that you will buy the new house when your current home sells and that kind of seals the deal of the new house being yours. With a foreclosure you can't do that. You have to sell the home that you currently live in and then purchase the foreclosure. I'm not knowledgeable enough in the real estate world to host a class or anything and I won't take up any more of your time trying to educate you on it but knowing how perfectly everything had to fall in to place is important to take note of here.

We got an offer on what was our current house and the rest was history. During that process I had found myself having pep talks with God. My prayers would go something like this, "God, I pray that your will be done through this. I know that if it is your will, you will make that my home God but if it isn't your will for me, can you make it your will for me?" Looking back, I can still feel the anxiousness I felt during that whole six weeks between the day we signed the contract and the day we closed.

Through this I learned that when God wants you somewhere, He will put you there. I would have never imagined living out in the country on that side of town but now that I'm there, you probably couldn't pay me to come back. We absolutely love it out there. I like to tell people it's like living on a farm without having to actually run the farm. God made everything that was involved in purchasing our sweet little one acre piece of property work out perfectly, and He reminds me of that every time I witness a sunset from my back porch.

It is amazing how much I've learned just by putting my attention into various things out there that I had never even noticed before. In the fall and winter months, I can watch the sun rise and sun set from my front porch. In the spring and summer months, I can watch the sun rise and set from my back porch. The timing of cows coming out to the pasture to eat is routine, which I can totally relate to that because I don't miss meals myself. The amount of stars I can see at night now that I'm out of the city seems like it quadrupled. The fall is absolutely gorgeous. Yellow, orange, and red trees line the hillside that's off in the distance in front of our house. All of these little things add up. They add up to a huge reminder of how amazing our God is and how incredibly huge this world is. It is a humble reminder of how small any problem that can arise in our life really is but even more importantly, how big our God is.

My thirtieth birthday was approaching quickly and would be here before I knew it so I was trying to prepare myself for this new decade I was about to step foot in to. I experienced so many emotions about this because this was my first birthday without having either parent to be here to spend it with me. Not to mention, this was going to be my first Christmas without them as well. So not only was I experiencing my first holidays and birthday without my dad and grand-father, I was also facing my first holiday season without any parents or grandparents. It was like all of my childhood memories of the holidays literally got put in a box and was put away. Yea, I still had the memories but I had lost the last two remaining members on both sides that always brought the memories of the past with them, through themselves. They kept me connected to those traditions if that makes sense. Though these feelings and emotions would come and go, I was pretty distracted by our big move.

I immediately started looking at thirty as an opportunity for growth and for big things for myself and my family. I no longer viewed this change as a process of me moving on in life without family that had passed away; I viewed it as a process of me, Ryan, and Laney moving on in life with each other. This was an opportunity for us to establish a life for us. We had this new house. We had this new way of life that we could create together, just three of us. We had each other. This was a new beginning for us and my perspective would be what set the tone for our future as a family. My husband and daughter were worth making sure it was a very positive perspective. They are my two primary sources where I see Jesus every day.

15

New Beginnings

Something amazing happens within you when you become a parent. I automatically wanted the best for Laney and I was on a mission to change whatever I felt the need to change within myself in order to create for her the best childhood and future. The first thing I realized that I needed to achieve was peace within me. I needed to learn how to love myself for exactly who I was and not just half way love me but completely and wholeheartedly love me. When we experience inner peace to its fullest potential it is amazing what we can do for the world around us much less our children and even ourselves.

In order to start this new journey, I first had to figure out what it was that was at that point, didn't contribute to a peaceful state of mind. I started reflecting on what it was about myself that I wasn't a huge fan of and the more I knit picked the things I didn't like about myself, the more I realized that those were the things that didn't bring me peace. When we don't like something and we have the capability to change it, we change it. Here I was, thirty years old, and about to make an attempt to change some things that had been a certain way for thirty years. This is when I quickly realized that it would be impossible for me to do that alone. These changes were necessary to accomplish my main goal of achieving pure peace. This was a nonnegotiable situation and it didn't take long for me to remember who carried me through those trips to the hospital to see my dad when cancer was spreading so quickly throughout his body. I remembered the peace that was gifted to me at a time in my life that I was terrified and felt so alone. Then I realized, that peace that I felt during some of the hardest times in my life wasn't a peace that I wanted to experience part time when times were the toughest and hardest. That was the peace that I wanted to experience every moment of my life. It was the peace that I wanted to feel during the good times and the bad times. It was the peace I wanted to feel through the easy times and the tough times. It was the peace that was required to change me. It was a peace that I knew without a doubt could be everlasting because God promises us that. It was a peace that is unachievable without God so I called on Him.

One thing I've learned about God is that He's always there waiting to hear from us. He's always there with His shoulder for us to lean on. He's always there with His arms wide open waiting to comfort us when we need Him. He's there in the middle of the night when our hearts are restless and we can't sleep. One thing a lot of us don't realize is that He's also there when we get that new job or when we get that promotion. He's even there when you reach that goal that you've worked so hard to achieve. And as much as we only have that desire to turn to Him, call upon Him, and pray to Him when what we are experiencing in life feels like the worst, one of His biggest desires for us is to also call upon Him when what we are experiencing in life feels amazing. He's a full time God and let me tell you, you need Him in this full time, ever changing world.

I do understand that it can be hard to feel, experience, and understand something or someone that we can't see or that we can't touch. Especially since we don't necessarily have someone physically here to tell us exactly how to start our own relationship and walk with God. It is just part of our human nature to not believe something until we see it but that's why God sent us Jesus so that we could see Him and we could believe in Him. God called upon the Disciples to start the sharing of the Good News and He used some of the most broken people to spread the word of the Gospel. He still uses broken people today and I know this because He's given me the gift of writing and has also gifted me with a faith filled life to write about.

Without Him I am broken but with Him I am fulfilled. He uses the broken so He can restore them and gift them with a life He has promised to us all. We are all broken in some type of way, shape, or form, but with the love from Him, we can be restored. He proves that over and over again as we glance at those among us who live a life filled with faith.

A little bit of each broken part of me and the things I had experienced in the past, contributed to the things that I realized didn't bring me peace. This process took a lot of self awareness for me and also quite a bit of praying for a changed heart. In order for us to recognize these things within ourselves and make ourselves aware of them, we have to get alone with God. We have to be still so that He can speak to our hearts. I was taking things I had viewed and experienced one specific way my entire life and praying for God to change my heart so that I could view them in the correct way according to His word. This process takes a lot of sacrifice and an endless amount of dying to our old ways. We have to surrender who we are in our flesh so that He can create in us who we are meant to be in the eyes of Him. He created each one of us and He created us in such a way that the peace our hearts long for is impossible without Him.

I understand that dying to ourselves and giving up who we are in our flesh does not sound appealing because well, it's not our way, and being in our flesh, we want everything to be our way. But we will never truly experience the peace God has promised us without actually giving up our old ways. The way I personally started to experience this change was through prayer. Any moment that I recognized I was going into a situation or a moment that had a tendency to leave me feeling uncomfortable, I would pray before that moment even came. We all have these moments and experience them often. Rather it was a moment that you have to interact with someone who treated you poorly or for me, going into an area that I would usually get claustrophobic, I would pray before that moment even came. If I was going to have to speak to someone I would pray for the words to speak to them. If I was going into an area I was usually claustrophobic in, I would pray for God to show me He was there. Any time we pray it immediately brings calmness to our moment. Even if we don't know what exactly to pray for, simply saying, "Jesus" will bring calm to our hearts.

After we become aware of the fact that we are truly trying to become more like Jesus, it is something that feels like it constantly remains on our conscience. Like anything else changing, over time, this will become an easier process that runs a little smoother once it is practiced more. The main thing to remember about life and our individual walks with God is that it will always be a battle. We will never come to a point in our lives that we will quit battling the things of this world so that Christ wins in our hearts. It will always be something that we have to work for and maintain. There will never be a time in our lives that it just happens naturally and falls right in our laps because with each battle we overcome, there will be another to come after that. It will always be that way until we get to heaven because there will always be things of this world that will try to attempt disturbing what we share in our hearts with the Spirit. That is called the enemy and once he is given even the tiniest opportunity to take over us, he will, and he will run ramped as long as we allow him to. I like to tell people that if there is ever a time that it doesn't feel like there's some type of battle happening in your life that's existing anymore then you are either in heaven or you have given up. As long as we are present here on earth, we will always be striving to get to our everlasting life with God in heaven so until we get there, we have to battle the things of this world. The beautiful thing about that battle though is that God is our battle partner and when we realize He's got us and every battle we will ever face here on earth, we've already won all the battles that we will ever face.

It is so important to realize that there will never come a time that you get to just stop trying. This world will never allow us to simply exist while everything in our lives take care of itself. God did not create us to just exist. He created each of us with a purpose. Even when we feel like we have no purpose at all, I can assure you that we do. I can assure you of this because you are still alive, breathing, and reading this book. This little reminder is for you. You may not be able to necessarily recognize even one purpose for you right now but I can assure you there's at least one because you're here.

There was once a point in my life I thought I didn't have a purpose. My mom who I was the caretaker of for many of years had passed away and once I lost her I felt as if I just existed. I got up and went to work every day and came home and drank most nights just to pass the time by. Looking back, I would have done completely different things with my spare time but I didn't know God like I do today so it was a good lesson for me. Little did I know that God would soon bless me with a beautiful baby girl and I would feel as if I had new purpose. The bottom line is that even through that year of me going to work and coming home and drinking, God still had purpose for me. I was still a wife. I was still a daughter. I was still a friend. I was still an aunt. I was still an employee.

We may not always be fulfilling a purpose that we had in mind for ourselves depending on which season we are in, but if we are alive and breathing, we are fulfilling a purpose for God. Sometimes, we aren't even aware of all of the impacts we make on a daily basis but there's purpose in every one of them. That's why we weren't created to simply exist and that's also why our walk with God is so important. Because every day we are here and we are consciously aware of God's existence and presence within us, we will continue to lead a life with purpose and even more importantly with a purpose that leads others to God.

16

Selflessness

One thing that I realized was that if I truly wanted to be more like Jesus, I had to love others like Jesus does. Well let me tell y'all, that part doesn't always come easy. It's hard to love the person that's obviously running late to something who just flew by me on the highway and shot an unkind gesture my way. It's hard to love the person who always snaps back with a negative comment which prompts me to nearly biting my tongue off in order to keep the situation peaceful. It's hard to love the person who is always grumpy and never smiles back when you smile at them. It's hard to love difficult people but more importantly, it's possible.

Honestly, there have been some moments in my own life that I have been difficult too. There were years in my own life that I was difficult to love. I was unhappy and thought the whole world was against me, but God still loved me through all of that and so did all of my friends and family. Obviously difficult people are dealing with difficult things. Jesus loves everyone no matter what they are going through. He's loved me through my roughest seasons and what's the most important about knowing that is that He loves me the same today as He did when I was hard to love. He has always loved me for who I am and for where I am and I can imagine that's how He wants us to love other people. Our first step in dying to ourselves is to love everyone He sends our way no matter how our flesh wants to react to the difficult ones. The difficult ones need Jesus' love the most so why not share that same love Jesus gives us all, through ourselves.

Love can be shared through numerous ways. It can be shared through forgiveness. Love can be shared through a smile. Love can be shared through listening to someone pour out their heart to you about something you don't understand. Love can be shared through giving your last bit of cash you have on you to the family sitting out in front of the grocery store waiting for the city bus to come. Love can be shared through a random text to friend to check on them. Love can be shared by complimenting the lady at the cash register who has maintained a smile as her line filled up with people who weren't very patient. Where there is love, hate cannot exist. Where there is love, there is Jesus. Sprinkle Jesus everywhere you go and when you make it a mission to do that, you will witness your life change.

Years ago these trendy bracelets came out that were must haves. I think most people just wanted them because they were the trend for that season but if I had to guess, a lot of people never even stopped and truly thought about what these bracelets meant or could mean for us. On the bracelets read, "WWJD?" The acronym stood for What Would Jesus Do? This simple phrase is gold. Imagine how often this phrase could be used in a day's time. Now imagine what amazing impact this world would have if every time this phrase was used, the present situation was then addressed in such a way that Jesus would address it. Wow, what a change we could make in this world? But for now, let the change start with you.

While learning to lead others to Jesus we learn that it is no longer about us. Slowly and organically, our life becomes centered on God, therefore everything we do and say becomes something that we are more conscience of. We don't just immediately respond to something that bothers us or threatens our ego, rather we think about it first; all the while sending prayers up to God as to how we respond or rather or not it even requires a response.

For me, one of the most challenging things to overcome was my ego. Our ego almost deafens our ability to hear anything else other than ourselves. Our ego always wants to be right. Our ego always wants to be heard and most definitely always wants the last word. Our ego is always in standby mode and ready to defend itself. When I came to know more about the love of Jesus and I was desperate to strengthen my walk in faith with God, I realized that in order for me to hear God at all, I had to learn how to hush my ego.

I think one reason we give up on pursuing anything is because it is so much easier than trying. Can you imagine changing the way you have been for your entire life? Well, if you can't, then I am here to tell you that it is nothing short of difficult. In some moments it can even become almost painful because you want to resort to the old way so bad. Why do we always want to resort to the old way though? Well, because it's much easier and takes a lot less work. But, we all know that if we want anything in life bad enough, the pain is worth it and eventually over time there will come the change.

It is kind of crazy looking back because initially I went into this trying to be a better example for my daughter. I didn't want her to struggle with the same things I have had to struggle with rather it be mentally or things of this world. I wanted to be able to help her with anything she ever came to me with and I wanted to be able to respond to her and her tough moments in the most patient and understanding way that I could. God led me straight to Him. Everything I wanted to be better for her for, required me to be a better and new and improved version of me. We start with improving ourselves through our relationship with God. We don't know what we don't know but through God, we can become everything we've ever dreamed of being and more.

Through this entire process I have come to realize that it's not even about me. It's about God. When we put Him first and have Him at the forefront of our brain, we are able to be exactly who He designed us to be. We come to know that we are of something higher than ourselves and we learn to share that with other people in how we respond to things of this world. In life we lead by example and the best way to lead others to God is to love them where they are and leave them better than they were when you found them.

I see this quote often and it goes like so, "Leave a little sparkle everywhere you go." When I see this quote or think of this quote I have an urge in my heart to replace sparkle with Jesus. If we sprinkle a little Jesus everywhere we go it will be impossible to leave any person in the same state that we found them. If we left a little Jesus there's no doubt we would leave them better than we found them.

When we are living a life for God we are truly living our best life. Life can never be better than a life that's lived for God and I know this because I have lived both. Without God we are empty and we are constantly in an attempt to fill ourselves with something of this world. That will never work though. God created us to be at a true state of peace through Him. He also sent us Jesus to be our connection to Him. He sent Jesus to lead by example. Jesus left the lives of those whose paths He crossed, better than he found them. He came to give us hope. He came to promise us a better life when we live it according to His word. Don't go another day thinking that you can achieve a better peace than the peace that God delivers us. It probably doesn't even sound normal to tell you that when I'm living my best life I am not putting myself first. But I am living proof that when I put God first, that's when my life is at its best, when it's not about me.

Sometimes our walk with God requires us to protect ourselves from the things and people that do not bring peace or joy to our lives. By all means, we can still treat others kindly, love them, and still sprinkle Jesus in their lives every time our paths cross but in order to protect ourselves from negative energy and the enemy, we have to put some distance there. In order to truly grow in our faith with God, we have to put boundaries up towards people and situations that we don't feel His presence in. I had a really hard time with this at first because a part of me felt guilty for abandoning things so to say. But once I experienced the peace I felt when I did come to God about those moments or those people, I knew that it was required for an even more strengthened walk in my faith. We can still love people and have boundaries. It's not about us, it's about God. If our walk with God strengthens when we learn to love some people at a distance because loving them and keeping them close threatens our inner peace, then we love them at a distance and that is okay. We grow closer to God when we learn to put boundaries between ourselves and anything that doesn't feel like it's getting us closer to Him.

When I realized this and I felt the peace that made me feel like this was actually okay, I experienced a sense of peace that I had never experienced before. For the first time in my entire life, I knew what was required of me to have a stronger relationship with God. It required me to establish some boundaries between me and anything that felt like it would disturb my focus on God. The enemy always shows up the most when we are attempting to grow in our faith. What we need to realize also is that we are in control of the amount of energy we put into things. If we are putting the majority of our energy into fighting the enemy rather it is through a person or a situation we are struggling with, we are depleting our energy source that we also use energy from to become strengthened in our faith. We can't do both. We have to leave the enemy where he stands and remember that God will take care of that. We then refocus our attention on God and put all of our energy into learning more about Him and establishing the bond that our hearts long for in Him.

We are here to carry out God's mission for our lives, and because of the focus that each one of our missions require we cannot be distracted by the enemy and the shenanigans he brings with him. Our focus should stay solely on God so that we can constantly stay connected to Him and be very presently aware of each new mission He's got planned for us. Because of the undivided attention that it takes for us to stay fully in the presence of God, boundaries are imperative to put up between us and any situation, or thought, or any person that the enemy attempts to get to us through. The simple gesture of creating boundaries can literally change your life.

17

Fear Is A Liar

One thing that most of my close friends and family will tell you about me is that in the past I have been known to be a people pleaser. I will admit that while I have had tendencies in the past of being exactly this, in my strengthening walk with God I have learned to transition from being a people pleaser if you will, to being a God pleaser. Believe it or not, both of these titles actually carry quite a few of the same tendencies. However, there is one main thing that comes to mind when I think about a major difference between the two. That major difference is that the people pleaser that in the past I would proudly raise my hand in being actually cared how other people viewed her decision making and the things about her. Now that I faithfully raise my hand high in pleasing God first and foremost, I have come to know that I am already loved and accepted by Him and with that I've learned to not make any decision in my life based on what someone else may think about my decision or about me at all.

When we see the world and everyone and everything operating around us, we realize that no one is really paying attention to us anyway. Everyone is pretty involved in their lives and not necessarily concerned at all actually with what we are doing in ours. All of this came to me at a time in my life I was thinking about making a big move, well for me it was big. As I was on the verge of turning thirty, I debated on starting a blog. I remember being so nervous about this and it was such a huge deal to me. Looking back, the only thing that was holding me back from actually going through with it and making it public was because I was in fear of what others would think about what I shared in my blog. For months I debated on this and went back and forth at how many people may think differently of me for sharing how I viewed experiences in my life. Would they think I was silly? Would they think I was crazy? Would they even read it? After praying really hard about this for weeks and praying about which direction I should go with it, one day it dawned on me that it didn't matter what anyone thought of my blog. If they didn't like it, they didn't have to read it. If they thought I was crazy or silly, well I didn't care about that either because like a light bulb, I remembered that I was already loved and accepted by God. What others think of me or what I do with my life was none of my business anyway. So what did I do that day? I became fearless.

So often we allow the fear of what someone else may think or what someone else may say control our next move. I don't think a lot of us realize what type of barrier we put on our own lives living like this. When we are living our lives with a filter based on other people, we aren't allowing the Spirit of God to work through us. You would be amazed at the amount of lives I touched through becoming fearless that day and creating that blog. God has been working through me every day since then. When we allow Him to work, He shows us that we can move mountains just simply remembering we are already fully loved and fully accepted by Him.

When you stop allowing other people to control you, rather it be through your response to their action or something as simple as allowing someone else to make you feel unworthy, that will be the day that you figure out how to battle fear. From that point on, you realize that in a moment that fear does attempt to reside in your mind rather it is through your own thought or from someone else, a quick reference of God's unconditional love for you will quickly armor you for the battle of whatever fear you are experiencing.

Something that I witness all of the time is that a lot of us don't even realize the type of power we are freely handing over to other people. There was definitely a time in my life that I allowed things to have more power and energy from me than I ever even should have. Something as simple as me smiling at someone and them not smiling back, yea I would let that negatively affect me. Honestly, I'm embarrassed to admit how much time I would spend wondering what it was that I did to them that would have kept them from smiling back. The most beautiful thing about that reaction process was that I had the power to change it.

There comes a time that we have to stop sharing our energy with things that don't make us feel good. Right now, think about things that don't make you feel good. I'm sure you can name quite of few of them. For me, waiting was one thing that didn't feel good while I did it. It could have been waiting for someone to call me back. I could have been waiting in line at a drive through. I could have been waiting for someone to show up at my house who said they would be there fifteen minutes earlier. While all of these things today may initially provoke a negative response, because well, that's human nature, I've also learned how to shut off the energy I feed it. When we don't feed negative energy, we take away its power. Do you know where to find power that's stronger than the negative thought, the negative situation, or the negative energy? That strong and mighty power my friend, is found in prayer. Prayer has by far been my biggest attribute in becoming fearless.

One of my favorite things to reference in a moment that I realize is making me feel even the slightest bit unhappy is this, "If it doesn't bring me peace or joy, then it's is not blessed by God." I don't know about you but I have to be honest, if it not blessed by God, then I don't want it to be a part of me. I don't want to allow it to have my energy. I don't want to allow it to affect me negatively in any way. When you place this type of filter on your life, it won't be long before you realize that we make life a whole lot more difficult than it's suppose to be. Another cool thing about this filter is that the more you use it, the more God uses you to positively impact other people who need Him to show up in their lives. He needs us all but more importantly He needs us all to have this type of filter so that we are less distracted by the things that keep us from seeing Him.

Something else I'm always in search of is truth. People say things that hurt us more often than they even probably realize. People use that as a defense mechanism for themselves and honestly, because of my history of experiencing death, this is something that I have never done simply because I know how quickly life can change. The last thing I want is for something to happen to someone I just attempted to break down with words. But I will be the first to admit that words are powerful and sometimes they really do hurt. I also realize that the people who use them to hurt us don't know any other way to comfort themselves and that's fine. But what a lot of people don't take into consideration that's on the receiving end of the words is that more often than not there's no truth in them. It's not always other people either delivering hurtful words to us. Often we are delivering them to ourselves and don't even realize it or at least realize that what we are telling ourselves isn't true. Look for the truth in what your own mind tries to convince you of too.

When we find the strength and ability to let go of anything and everything that we have ever allowed to hold our personal peace hostage, our hearts actually change.

What we often fail to realize though is how much control we do have in this. If we don't appreciate the way someone treats us, put distance there. If we feel uncomfortable when we are around a certain group of people, don't go anymore. If you are working somewhere that you dread going in to every day, apply at a new job. So often we are trying to fit in somewhere earthly but God needs us to stand out in our faith and we can't stand out in our faith while trying to fit in somewhere here on earth.

Through God we can find the strength to change anything our heart desires. You might say, "Well if I put distance there, it may hurt their feelings." or "If I don't go to those group events, they may not like me anymore or they may talk about me." I have two words for you, not to sound heartless but who cares? You will never get to where God has intended for you to be spiritually making decisions in your life based on someone else's feelings or opinions. Stop tip toeing around the people or situations that threaten your peace. Walk away from them while simultaneous still loving them because it is possible believe it or not. All things are possible with God.

The bottom line is this, there is absolutely nothing in this world that can leave you in any type of fear that God can't comfort you through and provide you the strength to overcome. Where faith is, fear cannot exist. Do not spend another moment of your life being in fear of a person, a situation, a thought, or a possibility. Do not go another day being held captive to fear. Go for that goal.

Accomplish that dream. It is very important to remember that if someone judges it or comments on it in any other way than an uplifting and positive way, well then it's a good thing that they are your dreams. You are becoming fearless and their negative comments can't affect you because God has already blessed those dreams and planned for them to come into existence. He did that the day that He laid them on your heart.

18

Let It Be

I once asked my husband what his favorite quality about me was. A lot of times when a woman asks their husband or their significant other this particular question, like me, they are probably thinking the answer is going to be some type of body part. It's natural to expect this response right? Well that day my husband completely blew my mind because it wasn't at all a body part that was his favorite quality. He said, "My favorite quality about you babe is acceptance. No matter what life has ever handed you, you've accepted it." Y'all, I had tears well up in my eyes when he said this. For one I wasn't expecting that to be his answer at all so I was totally surprised by it. For two it just goes to show how much people notice about what's inside of us.

Acceptance is one very important key factor in experiencing God on an intimate level and putting your faith and trust in Him at its highest. In one single day, think about how many things you want to go your way. You want the light to stay green because you are running late. You want there to be no line at the coffee shop so you can swing through there, grab your coffee. You want there to be zero traffic so you can roll into work on time with one minute to spare because you are on a mission to get that employee of the month title. You want the kids to come home in the afternoon with smiles. You want to come home and your significant other to have cooked dinner and have all the plates made and the laundry done. I mean, we all know the list is endless because we are human and we want everything always working in our favor. Guess what, everything will not always work in our favor. These ideas of a perfect day, a perfect life, or a perfect world, please do me a favor right now and kiss them goodbye. Let me be real with you for a moment, it will never exist. There's no such thing as perfect and there is no way that every day of your life everything will always go your way.

Now, because you have set your day with all of the expectations, any of these things that don't go your way does have the capability to change your whole tone for the day. You catch every red light on the way in, the line at the coffee shop is wrapped around the building, and because those two things have put you behind, you are now sitting in a school zone behind a bus full of kids you don't know, feeling very aggravated, and also wondering why they don't start school later than during the window of time you have to be at work. There may or may not be colorful words being thought or even said aloud at this point because this makes three situations that have not gone your way. So, from the time you walked out of the house this morning with a smile and a little piece of encouragement to yourself, "It's going to be a great day."

to the time you arrived at your desk, your negative energy level has gone from zero to one-hundred. So not only do you have to fake a smile to all of your coworkers, you also have taken every situation you've encountered prior to now and unconsciously made it negative because it didn't go your way. One little change could have turned your whole morning around and could have made a huge difference in the entire outcome completely. That little change would have been your ability to accept all of your inconveniences just as they were. Instead, at this point, you have allowed them all to become negative in your mind and now you've allowed them to set the tone for your day.

My dear friend that I work with who I mentioned earlier in a previous chapter, that has been such a blessing to my life, said something to me one day and it just stuck. He said that he thinks of my motto as being, "Let it be." It's funny because that day I cornered my husband and asked him what his favorite quality about me was and he responded with, "Acceptance" and then I have one of my favorite humans telling me that, "Let it be" is my motto. So with these two things I want to tell you this, that in order to be able to accept things, you have to just let them be. Nothing ever has to be good or bad to us and if it is, we are the ones putting the label on them. Just let things be. In order to begin your own personal walk with God, you have to start here. You have to accept anything life hands you, rather it be every red light on the way to work or that job you applied for that you wanted so bad, fell through. You have to learn to accept what you feel is going against you just as easily you accept what you feel is going for you. This is what I use the most to keep my faith strengthening in God, my husband's favorite quality.

After we are able to accept the things we feel are for us or against us equally, we learn to appreciate them equally. God never does anything in our lives to harm us. I have learned that no matter what happens in my life, even if my flesh initially wants to define something as being negative, God has promised me that nothing that happens in my life happens to harm me.

I had experienced the loss of both of my parents before my thirtieth birthday. Obviously this is something that is very devastating. Do you know what I do every single day though at some point? I thank God for the time He allowed me to have with them. I thank Him for the years I was able to spend with them and all of the cherished moments I will never forget. I would give anything to have them back here but the reality is that I never will. Yes, I could spend every day sad and wondering why they died so young. I could question Him as to why He chose my parents to go but I don't. I think a lot of us fail to realize how short our time really is here. Let's spend more time bringing joy to others lives. If I spent all of my time being sad about something I couldn't change, I'd never be able to make a positive impact on the lives of those who God brings across my path. God didn't send me here to tell you a story about me being upset with Him because He needed my parents back before I turned thirty years old. God sent me there to tell you about how He's brought me through it.

Death is an extremely hard thing for any human to experience, much less accept. We don't want someone that we love to be gone; we want them here with us. A lot of us don't understand why God chose someone we love and that meant so much to us versus someone somewhere else. We selfishly would rather it be someone else than a loved one of our own but God just don't work that way. The day God created us He had a mission in mind for each and every one of us, and so once we have fulfilled our mission He brings us back to be with Him at our everlasting home in Heaven. That's why He encourages us to live spiritually instead of solely in our flesh. As long as we are living spiritually, we realize that at any time, any one we love can be called back home and it comforts our heart in knowing they are with Him and we will see them again when our own mission has been accomplished.

Once we change our perspective and learn how to accept and appreciate things just as they come to us we gain a whole new understanding. We know that anything that happens in our lives is never done to us to make us sad or unhappy. We are faced with tough obstacles and tough experiences in order to be able to prosper. Every time we experience one of these situations and we put all of our faith in God and rely on Him to help us get through it and trust that He is always in control, through that, we are given hope.

Through prayer and steadfastness in my faith I have learned to change even the smallest things that I didn't even realize at the time, made such a huge impact on me. I have learned to say or think to myself instead of, "Why is this happening to me?" to "This is happening for me." Honestly, most of the time, I have no idea why it's happening for me in that moment, especially if it is something that doesn't seem to be in my favor. But you know who does? God and He can see the future and He knows how this moment that for me right now feels inconvenient and not exactly in my favor, will be beneficial to my future self. Every tough situation that we are ever faced with is a building block to our strength and wisdom and they provide growth to us for our future missions He has in store for us. The more we rely on Him in those trials and moments of our lives, the more we are able to trust Him and His plan for us. This is how He equips us to be able to help others and help lead others to Him. He encourages us to have child like faith. In the same way that we prep our children for their future, He preps us for ours.

19

Love Wins

One of the greatest gifts that I could have ever received from my parents was their love. Both of them were such loving parents and it wasn't just an, "I love you" when we hung up the phone or a, "Love Always" at the bottom of a birthday card, it was a very genuine love that they both were able to express through their actions so naturally. That is such a gift. It is a gift that this world desperately needs. While not everyone may have received a love as compassionate and as fulfilling as I did from my parents, there is still opportunity to be loved by someone that already unconditionally loves us all. The only thing keeping you from experiencing that is you.

If people could make love their first impression toward another individual that they're meeting for the first time, think of how impactful that would be for the world. Instead unfortunately so many people allow what someone looks like on the outside to be their first impression of that individual. So what that means immediately is that your heart and mind has already shut them out from even a conversation because of their appearance. In order to accept any person or anything, you have to love them first. You have to love like Jesus does and we all know Jesus loves everyone.

As we all know, there are plenty of things that we don't agree on. There are plenty of issues that not everyone has the same approach to solving. One person may go to a church that has a specified denomination while another may go to a church that is nondenominational. Politics is a popular place for different views and different opinions as well. Growing up I always heard, "Politics and religion is something you just can't discuss." I guess people think if they argue long enough they could change someone's mind, but we all know how that works. It doesn't. Please save that energy for something else. I'm not a real opinionated person myself but at the end of the day, in my opinion, it doesn't seem like it really needs to be discussed anyway. People will argue and say some of the most terrible things about both of these topics and even sometimes about a person who believes one way or the other, simply because it is different than their own belief or opinion. But at the end of the day, we're all the same in the eyes of God. We shouldn't only allow ourselves to love people because they live the same way we do or believe the same things we do. We are encouraged to love everyone just the way they are, beliefs and all. God says to just love them, He'll sort them out later.

Something that really bothers me that I have picked up on in my journey through life is that if someone who believes in God finds out that someone they are associating with doesn't believe in God, they turn their back and cut ties. We will never be able to bring others to God that doesn't already believe in Him if we disassociate ourselves with them. How else will they ever learn about Him? We are here to be the hands and feet of Jesus and I know without a doubt that Jesus' feet didn't flee the scene when He approached a nonbeliever. Love a nonbeliever just as much as you love your preacher and watch God work His miracle through you.

We also can't share the Lord with others by forcing it on them. It's not a bartering system. We can't lead people to believe that if they would be believers or come to church, we will love them more. That seems to be the approach that a lot of people take when it comes to religion and I have to be honest, it probably scares people away. I think if we could just love people how they already are no matter what they believe or may not believe, we've already given them a glimpse of God just by loving them. I'm a firm believer in actions speaking louder than words. I think if we can just simply let others witness what God is doing through us we will be more likely to lead others to Him by sharing His love through us, with them.

You may be someone who argues or wants to get the last word. You may be someone who turns your back on nonbelievers. You may be someone who immediately categorizes someone because of what they look like or what they are wearing. But guess what, God loves those people just as much as He loves you. He loves an inmate as much as He loves a police officer. He loves someone who is struggling with drugs as much as he loves someone sober. He loves the drive through worker as much as he loves the owner of the company the drive through worker is employed at. We don't get to heaven by being perfect and not associating with people who aren't like us. We get to heaven through our own personal walk with God and that involves loving others for where they are. God is love and every time we express love we bring Him to the moment.

We are all on separate journeys and each of our journeys move at a different pace. When I think of what our paths look like intertwined through one another, I imagine a road map. God knew what He was doing when He made each one of our paths and also the timing of everyone that has crossed them. I'm always in amazement at the perfection of the timing of when He brings people across my path or me across someone else's. Rather they come and stay or rather they come and go, they all serve a purpose and when you look at it in hindsight, it will blow your mind. Try it!

When we love God first, we gain a whole new perspective on how to love others for being who they already are without wanting to change everything we don't agree with about them or their lives. We don't have to agree with people to love them. There will be some that may be harder to love than others and I've realized that those are the ones that need love the most. What really helps me when God intertwines my path with someone's that may initially seem a little more difficult to love, is remembering that they are a child of God just like me so they deserve to be loved just as much as I do. So with that, I love them anyway. I also realize that the only way they will ever come to know the Lord is through someone that shows them love like Jesus would if He was here. Well, I guess technically He is here. He is here in each one of us. That's why He uses those of us who have already gone through our season of knowing Him at a more in depth level to positively impact the lives of those who haven't had their season yet. He's pretty genius like that. He's using us to help start their season so don't pass up the opportunity to help someone else become love.

When we are attempting to enter this new season of our own and we are trying to become a more faith filled follower of God, it requires so much change within ourselves and let me tell you something, it's definitely not an overnight type of change. We have to literally shut our flesh down and stop allowing it to control who we are. This is the point where God steps in and fills your life with him. This is the point that you get to see and experience freedom for yourself when you love God first.

Rather you are a, "Do good for others and good will come to you." type of person or a "What would Jesus do?" type of person, both requires us to not live in our own flesh. Our flesh and our ego have tendencies to mislead us to treat others the way that they treat us but the two prior quotes I listed remind us to not do that. Both quotes lead us in the direction of love and if we are headed in the direction of love or leading others in the direction of love through our actions, then we are constantly being the hands and feet of Jesus. Some of us realize we are sharing Jesus and some of us don't. Rather we realize it or not, isn't the point here. The point here is to point out to you that in everything done in love brings God into the moment. The more love we share the more we will bring God to the center of not only our lives, but also into the lives of others.

Love requires understanding. Love requires us to understand that because we may be where we are today in our own journey, we don't disregard someone else's whereabouts in their journey just because they aren't quite where we are. We have to be humble enough to remember that there was a time in our own lives that we sat right where they are. There was a time in my life that I admired anyone that could faithfully follow Christ without allowing anything in this world to affect them. We can't roll our eyes at the Christians who go to church every Sunday but still don't live a life like Jesus. We can't put someone down for not living this ideal life of what we believe they are supposed to. God didn't send us here to do that. He sent us here to be understanding and to love people anyway. Love them beyond their mistakes. Love them beyond their poor choices. Love them beyond their own demons.

I've been a Christian my entire life and I spent a lot of those years judging others if you want me to be honest simply because they did things differently than I did. But I learned to stop judging people when I experienced something in my life that I would have never imagined experiencing as a child and that was my mom's addiction. I had this wonderful and amazing mother who was any child's dream mom if there ever was such a thing. She was so compassionate and so genuine in everything she did. The light she radiated toward every single life she touched shined as bright as the sun. But something happened in her life and it pretty much darkened every bit of that light that ever shined. Yea she would have days where she would seem to be a little happier than others but since the day her mom had died, she struggled to ever face obstacles head on. Any upcoming experience that brought any type of fear or anxiety would leave her almost paralyzed in her ability to function in daily life. Of course along with this, came depression and depression isn't just any typical disease. It is a disease that can literally suck the life you've always known in a person completely out. After experiencing something that hit so close to home for a solid thirteen years I came to realize that anything can happen to anyone.

This experience humbled me and it really showed me how to be understanding to people no matter what they were battling in their own lives. Just because someone is struggling with addiction today, doesn't mean they weren't at some point in their life an amazing mother who didn't miss a field trip with their daughter. Just because I'm a faithful follower of Christ today doesn't mean that at some point in my life I wasn't sitting back passing judgment about someone else. We are all guilty of coming up with our own ways of correcting someone's life style or being tempted to show a parent how to discipline their own child. We're human. We want everyone to be like us and we are so quick to not accept them if they aren't. But if we could just understand that we are all on different journeys fulfilling different missions at different times for God, we would realize that the best things we could do for anyone who He sends across our path is to love them and love is one of the main requirements for being understanding.

Love also requires kindness. Kindness is the quality of being friendly, generous, and considerate. A lot of times, kindness can be found in a moment of selflessness. Our ego constantly tries to convince us to make everything about us but to love others; we have to stop thinking about ourselves so much for a change. We have to learn how to be compassionate and to take into consideration the emotions and feelings of others. We don't have to agree with people to be kind to them.

If you feel like I'm talking directly to you, then I think probably a good place to start to practice more kindness is toward yourself. Sometimes the unkind things we hear are from ourselves. But if you could figure out how to love yourself more knowing you are unconditionally loved by God and treat yourself more kindly, it would be easier for you to share kindness with other people. A lot of times, we show the world what goes on within us simply by how we treat others. Don't feel alone here because there was a time in my life that kindness wasn't the first thing on my mind either. It was a comfort zone though and in order to grow and change, we have to rely on God to help us overcome them. There is no better time than the present to make it a point to love more. Love conquers all and I can assure you that God plans to conquer quite a bit through you with love being His main source.

20

Heart Of Gratitude

As we all are already aware of, life is short. It is always so difficult to grasp that and honestly, for me, it's never flown by faster since I hit the age of twenty-five. It was like the speed of the years doubled and then tripled once I had my daughter. I see so many of us usually looking forward to stuff rather it's a vacation we planned or for most of us it's the weekend. If I can imagine why a lot of people seem to be looking forward to particular moments like the weekend and vacation it is because they know those moments are going to make them happy once they get there. I got news for you though; we don't have to wait to experience joy. Don't waste another moment waiting to feel joy.

I see people who think they will be happy when they find a new job. I see other people who think they will be happy when they pay off their debt. I constantly witness people who think that they will be happy when they get a new car. I see people who think they will be happy when they come home to a spotless house. I've been one of these people myself in the past but if you will notice, all of these scenarios that people think once they have overcome they will be happy, are all scenarios that people are placing their happiness in the hands of something else. They are giving something else other than themselves the power to determine their happiness and they are putting their joy in a future matter. Happy doesn't start when we pay off every bill we have. Happy doesn't start when we finally move to a new home. Happy doesn't start once you've finally gotten that new technical device that you've been waiting so long to be released. Do you know when happiness starts? It starts with joy. And joy starts the day that you learn to appreciate and enjoy what you already have.

On countless occasions I witness people thinking that once they do this or don't do that then they will be happy but that's just not how life works. We can't place something so important and so crucial to exist within us in hopes to make the world a better place, in the hope of something in the future. We need to understand what it takes to feel joy today. Today, the only thing that is in control of your joy is you.

It is quite often that being happy and being joyful get tossed in the same category. I have to disagree here though because I think you have to be joyful to truly be happy. To be joyful, you have to be grateful and you have to know how to express gratitude. When we are full of joy, chaos can erupt around us and we still have the ability to see the things to be grateful for in the midst of the chaos. While we may not necessarily be happy in that specific moment, we can still have joy. Joy is a state of our being.

Being joyous is a state in our mind that we do have control over. We can still see all the good amongst what looks to be bad. To become joyful, we need to become optimistic. To become optimistic, we need to change our mind.

Our minds are quite powerful and I allowed mine to completely control my life for years. It felt like it was wired at birth to point out the negative or worst case scenario in every situation. Even to this day, it will find a way to creep back into my mind but this brings me back to what I stated in a previous chapter, about always being on the lookout for truth. I've learned that most negative thoughts aren't true and the immediate moment that I realize this in any situation, I replace that energy that my brain wanted to use in feeding the negative thought, with energy toward a positive thought. Initially this is tough. Especially if you are like me at all and you have spent years and years immediately thinking negative in anything. Most negative thoughts disturb our inner peace so we have to nip them in the bud. Remember, what one of my favorite phrases is, "If it doesn't bring us peace or joy then it isn't blessed by God."

Overtime this process will become easier and in the beginning you will have every urge to give up trying because it takes a lot of work and a lot of discipline but I promise it will be worth it. It will be worth it for you. It will be worth it for your children. It will be worth it for every person's life you touch on a daily basis. I feel so much better now that I am able to find the positive in absolutely every single situation I witness. Especially since at one point in my life I only knew how to find the negative. I often hear people comment on how positive I am and honestly, they have no idea how much of an uphill battle it was to get here. In a world full of constant things that it's in our nature to be brought down by, there is no other word to describe overcoming that except for difficult. I kept feeling like I was failing every time I would give in to my old way of processing things. But there is one thing I can assure you of and that is that God will give you the strength to do it and the grace for the moments you feel as if you failed.

Nothing has ever pushed me to make a change more than my daughter did. I don't want her to ever have to face the same struggles that I have had to and had I not made an attempt to change some of the things I was not at all a fan of about myself, it could have become a learned behavior for her. Rather it was how I hollered at the car that pulled out in front of me, how someone approached me in a negative manner and the way I responded to them, or even just a small complaint about something, these can all become learned behaviors. Our kids are always watching us and they learn so much from us. I am by no means perfect nor have I ever led myself or anyone else to believe that. I'm human. I will tell you every flaw that I have ever had and I am humble enough to tell you that. People laugh when I tell them that I have grown up with her, but in all seriousness, I have. There has been so much about myself that I have worked extremely hard to change in order to be a better example for her. Being positive is important. Finding joy in the midst of anything is important.

It amazes me because initially, I went into this huge change just wanting to be better equipped for her. I quickly learned though that I had to help me first before I could ever even think about being able to help her and her future self. Beautifully enough, in parallel to becoming a better mom and learning how to deal with moments and ways of thinking completely different than how I ever had, God has taught me how to rely on Him through the times when we feel like we can't be helped. There is no doubt in my mind that God had everything to do with the timing of when He gifted me with her. He knew what all He was about to change within me all the while He knew how effective that change would be for those whose paths would come across mine.

We think we are stuck in these ways and the reality is that we do have the capability to change them but it takes more than just ourselves. We tend to forget that through the message of the Bible God tells us exactly where to come when we are weary and faint. He tells us where to come when we feel like giving up. He tells us where to come for truth. Every single time I found myself in a moment that I wanted to respond in an old way, through prayer He gave me the ability to respond in a new way more aligned with how He showed us to be through His only son Jesus.

God's way is love, joy, peace, patience, kindness, goodness, faithfulness, gentleness, and self-control. If there is ever none of these in a moment, simply pause and pray. If you feel as if you have an urge to respond to something in such a way that doesn't involve one of these, pause and pray. In order for us to allow God to work through us and change our hearts, we have to change our minds and allow Him to do so. We have to learn how to just give up control and give all of the control to Him. I promise you, He knows what He's doing. I have lived a life without Him and I have lived a life with Him and I can assure you my life has never been in more of a state of peace than it is today. I love it because no matter how much we acknowledge His presence He is always just a prayer away. He is always with us. He never leaves us and He always meets us at the most devastating moments of our lives regardless of how much we made it a point or lacked in making it a point to reach out to Him prior to that devastating moment.

Joy begins with you and if you feel too empty to pursue it, God is right there with you waiting for you to call upon Him for help. Don't spend another day being held at the mercy of things and people of this world. Don't spend another day thinking that you will find joy when you get that new house or find you will find joy in a significant other. Start getting filled with joy today. I can assure you it's not just a switch you can turn on it takes more than just a simple change of mind. It takes continuous prayer. It takes discipline and strength and courage. It took more than who I knew how to be by myself. It took the power of God to help me change from who I was in the flesh to who I have become in my faith.

One thing I want you to be sure you do before you even start in on praying for God to help you change your heart and to help you change your way of thinking, and that is that I want you to thank Him for what He has already gifted you with. When we can be grateful for every single thing that we already have and we can be grateful for every single thing that we have experienced no matter how high our highs were or how low our lows were, we feed our mind joy. There's something about expressing gratitude for what we already have that opens up a whole new window of opportunity in the pursuit of a positive change in our lives and our way of thinking.

I'm grateful for my entire life. I'm grateful for all of the highs and the lows. I'm grateful for the tough times and I'm grateful for the easy times. I'm grateful for the time He gifted me with my parents. I'm grateful for all of the heartache I experienced in becoming a mother and everything it took to have a successful pregnancy. I'm grateful for a husband who works hard every day and comes home and loves his girls. I'm grateful for the health of my family and the jobs that my husband and I have that give us the ability to come home and put food on our table. I'm grateful for a roof over our head and the love that my family shares together under that roof. There's something about being grateful that triggers the emotion of joy.

It is so discouraging and sometimes can even be dangerous for us to allow something or someone outside of our own being to decide rather or not we are going to feel joyful or not. With that being said stop waiting to be happy. Stop putting your joy on hold until things go your way. Be joyful today, in a chaotic world where so much tends to have the capability to bring us down. When you become full of joy, you become full of love. When you become full of love, you start positively impacting lives of those who surround you. When you start positively impacting the lives of those who surrounds you, you turn peoples head in the direction of God. When you turn peoples head in the direction of God, you are fulfilling His purpose for your life. When you are fulfilling His purpose, He keeps you filled up. I'm sure you are curious as to what He keeps us filled up with and the answer to that my friend is joy, which constantly fulfills us with Him.

21

Living Spiritually

Obviously we know that God is always present with us but when we can't see something physically present in front of us with our own eyes, we tend to forget that it is existent within us every single moment. Without even realizing it, sometimes we allow the world to consume us with all of its troubles because that's what is directly in front of us and that's what we see. It's difficult to always stay constantly connected to God without letting everything that exists directly in front of us interfere with our relationship with God. We're human and He gets it. I think that's why He organizes things in such a methodical fashion.

Have you ever experienced a moment that happened perfectly in your life? One of those moments that it just felt meant to be and the timing was so perfected that it left you speechless. That's Him. Those are the moments that I can often be found using the quote, "It's a God thing." Those moments are the moments that leave your mind blown without any other explanation other than God because it was so perfectly aligned that it couldn't have possibly been explained any other way.

I feel like God places little reminders like those throughout our lives in hopes that we see Him. Those little things and moments that require us to see things beyond the surface of what they look like to the flesh. It could be at a time you are feeling lonely or abandoned and out of nowhere a friend calls or texts to check on you. It could be in the form of a message on a church sign. It could be in the form of a fish emblem on the trunk of a car with a tiny cross in the center of it. It could be in the form of a Bible verse on a pen that you used to sign your name at the convenient store. The possibilities are endless but never miss an opportunity to acknowledge Him and recognize His presence when He shows up. You may be wondering, "How in the world does something that seems so normal in our day to day travels make her reference God?" Well, remember when I first started in my attempt to digging deeper in my faith? It was during that season of my life that I started praying for the eyes to see Him. Since then, He's literally become so big in my life, I can't miss Him.

One specific moment that I am able to recognize Him in every single time is when I am spending time with my daughter. When I set the entire world on the back burner and shut out anything that could keep me distracted from her and I give her my time, He gives me Him through her. I've noticed that He is most present when we are most present. The only place we can be most present in is a moment that's happening right now. We can't be thinking about yesterday's problems or the possibilities of tomorrow and still live fully present in the now. God is most obvious in children and through them, they keep us connected.

In a previous chapter I mentioned how much I love sunsets and sunrises. I envision a sunrise as an opportunity to start a day directly with God. Nothing else comes to mind other than God and another day that I have opportunity to share Him with others. It's a sweet little reminder that He's still using me and He still needs me here. I have been known to be layered up and in a robe, with a cup of coffee on a Saturday or Sunday, sitting on my front porch in a rocking chair spending time with God through a sunrise. Try it. It will change the tone for the whole day.

Sunsets though, a sunset is a gentle reminder that I've gone through another day, sharing Him through me and everything about Him that exists in me has gone yet another day being shared with other people. I bet when my husband was building my daughters play ground fort he had no idea I would be using it just as much. She and I have been known to go sit up in that to experience a sunset while having a tea party. Let me tell you something, there is nothing sweeter and not a moment in my life that I experience God any more deeply than a moment with my child and a sunset.

Set time aside to notice the things that so many in this world don't notice. When I witness a sunrise or a sunset it reminds me of how incredibly huge this world is. It reminds me of how amazing and phenomenal our God is. He is a powerful God. In some way, shape or form, He created every single bit of everything that exists here. A big sunrise or a big sunset will always have the capability of bringing us back to how small our day to day, worldly problems are. They are absolutely nothing at all when they are set next to our big God.

This season of life will come to you in God's perfectly designed time for you. This season will be one that for the first time in your whole life you actually appreciate a sunrise or a sunset. You will realize that the cows come to the same part of the pasture at the same time every day to graze. You will find a deeper meaning to the horses that you pass every day that are always gathered together in the beautiful rolling hills of the countryside. You will piece together all of these little moments and will reference every one of them back to one big God. It will be during this season of your life that you are connected with God on the level He anticipates everyone to get to when He creates us. He designs all of these little temporary, yet miraculous things and these moments to keep us connected to Him and on the road back to our eternal life with Him in heaven. This will be the season that you realize that you don't stay connected to God through anything material. You stay connected to God through moments. The moments are what fill us up and we have to be full to be able to help fill others. Figure out where you feel God's presence the most and do more of that.

One week before my mom died I got a tattoo that reads, "Cherish Every Moment." At the time I just wanted to get a tattoo because I was twenty-five and had still never gotten a tattoo. Since I can remember it had always been my favorite quote but at that time in my life, I honestly wasn't sure how to truly cherish a moment. Fast forward until today I make it a point to truly live in and cherish moments. I guess because of the loss I have experienced in my life, it has been an unconscious change within me. I think I am just able to realize that in the blink of an eye our entire world can change.

I've witnessed my mom struggle with addiction for thirteen years and then in one single night, by accident, she overdid it. I've witnessed my dad go from being perfectly healthy to having a time line put on his life when he was told he only had a year or less to live. I've witnessed three heartbeats that existed inside of me just stop between one doctor's appointments to the next. I've witnessed every single one of my grandparents have their life taken by illness, three of which were put on a time line and the last one was sudden. I've witnessed my uncle who I never knew to struggle with anything drink too much one night, made a choice he wouldn't have made sober, and never wake up the next day. I've witnessed my aunt whose life was tragically taken in a car accident two weeks after my dad died, on the same exact day my grandfather died. Perhaps a little bit from each experience impacted me big. That big impact was to truly cherish moments. That big impact was being able to recognize a perfectly present God in those truly cherished moments.

A constant joy will not be found in material things. Yes, material things may bring you temporary joy like the latest released phone or a new pair of shoes but they will never provide to you the endless and everlasting joy that God brings us. The only way of receiving that continuous joy from God is through moments.

I've noticed this trend with myself and I'm unashamed to share it with you. I started this trend right after my mom died. It picked right back after my dad died. And believe it or not I have been found to also be doing this during the holiday season. I shop a lot and by shop I don't mean a little something here and a little something there. By shop I mean, shop until my future self that I eventually meet up with drops at how much money I blew. I'm surely grateful for my awareness at the end of the shopping adventure but I'll always be wondering where in the world was that awareness tucked away and hiding at in the beginning?

As I look back at these impulse shopping sprees that I thought during the time were fulfilling I realize one very obvious thing and that is that I had gotten a little distant from God. Most of us tend to do that in times that we need Him the most. We go back to the familiar and the look for the things physically present that can bring us comfort and joy during the time we need it. These are all seasons of my life that were a little more painful than the others and instead of filling my life with more of Him I was filing my wardrobe with things I would probably change my mind about by the next month. These sprees always seem fun and fulfilling in the moment but by the end of them I'm able to recognize that I was seeking comfort from somewhere else other than God during the time I needed His comforting the most. That somewhere else was in something material that is only temporary. I've pep talked myself into being better at seeking God who is found in moments and who is eternal. I realize that I can be fulfilling my heart with Him and comforting my hurt through moments that involve Him.

I don't know where you go or what you may do when your heart is hurting or you feel as if you need to be comforted. For some it may be found in alcohol or medication. For some it may be going to an ice cream shop or going to a bar. For some it may be found in shopping like it is for me. I want you to realize something about all of these things and that is that they are all temporary comforts. They are all temporary fixes. In all of these examples we are relying on something of this world to provide temporary comfort or joy to us when we have the option to rely on someone eternal and everlasting to comfort us. It is through the process of realizing that we are using temporary things to comfort us and bring us joy and that we need to rely less on them and more on God, that we start realizing that He exists in moments.

22

Rooted in Faith

So much has changed within me in the past year. In one year alone God has spread through my heart like wildfire. I can't help but to thank Him for allowing me the opportunity to move to a side of town I was unfamiliar with that I would have never dreamed of moving to because it was out of my comfort zone. There is no doubt in my mind that He knew that view would seal the deal on the purchase. Ever since my dad had gotten sick, I had fallen in love with sunsets. They always gave me such a deeper sense of self. I would chase one all over town just to find a good spot to experience it in and I have to be honest that while I found some pretty cool spots, I had never found a perfect one. Little did I know God already had the perfect one in store for me. He had it planted right at the beginning of my faith flourishing journey with Him, from my very own porch.

I have to say that if I would have just stuck with my routine flesh ways of doing things and passed up the opportunity to trust Him as He led me in the unfamiliar, I know without a doubt I wouldn't be where I am today in my faith journey. This was huge for me to agree to move to a place well out of my comfort zone but through this,

God has shown me that He's bigger. God will never be able to move through us if we don't allow him to and in order to allow Him, we have to give up control. Faith is complete trust or confidence in someone or something and you have to be sure that your faith is bigger than your fear. Through this very experience I learned that when God sees a future that we can't, He is able to send us into moments and into situations that play a small part in changing our hearts and also changing that bigger picture that we can't see at the precise moment. This showed me that the wilderness season is the same season that's meant for our faith to be deepened.

When we give God control of things, we are able to let go of the idea that we have control to begin with. There's really not much here on earth that we are able to control anyway even though we lead ourselves to believe that. However we do have the ability to control ourselves and how we respond to things so the next time you realize something outside of your control has disappointed you, change the way you look at it. Don't look at it as it being a disappointment. Instead, look at it as being God's will. When we know that God's will is constantly being done in our lives and we are accepting of that even though our flesh didn't necessarily want it to be that way, a peace will come over you and trust me, there is nothing on this earth that can compare to that peace God gifts us. It's totally worth it to give up control and trust His will.

Trusting God's will has given me the ability to not worry about things. God has shown me time and time again that worrying about anything is a waste of energy. Let's start using that energy we use to worry about things we have no control over anyway, toward prayer to someone who already knows what the future looks like. I can picture God sitting up in heaven like, "I don't know why in the world they are down there worrying about things that I already know the outcome of. I wish they would just put their faith in me and trust that my will, will be done so that they can experience true inner peace." No matter how much we ever worry, y'all we will never change the outcome of whatever it is we are worrying about. Spend that time strengthening your faith in the Lord in some type of way rather than distancing yourself from Him by worrying.

Speaking of worry let me talk to you a little bit about worry. One thing I don't worry about anymore is what people think of me. You see before God sends us out on missions He equips us with courage and confidence. It's a gift that He's sure we have before He sends us out into a world that is filled with opinions and judgment. When you realize that you are completely loved and accepted by God it provides armor for you that no one anywhere can get through. It doesn't matter what they say or what they may think of you. If you know you are serving your life for the purpose of fulfilling God's purpose for your life, you are untouchable and even more importantly, God creates you to be unstoppable. I used to stand in my closet spending a ridiculous amount of time trying to pick out the perfect outfit for the day. Hoping no one said anything to me to make me feel any more uncomfortable than what I may have already felt. I felt like I needed someone else's opinion of rather or not it looked okay. There was a time or two I even brought an extra shirt or an extra pair of shoes along in case whoever I decided to ask didn't confirm it for me. You know what I don't need anymore? I don't need confirmation. I don't need confirmation because God already loves me no matter what I decide to wear each day. Appearance doesn't define who we are, our hearts do.

I think a lot of people get caught up in being way too involved in what other people think of them based on their appearance. I witness so many people being competitive and comparing themselves and their own journeys to others but God didn't have this in mind at all when He designed us. Just to bring it into perspective, think about all of the different career options that are available to us. Now just pick one of those careers off of the list that you thought of and think about all of the different skills that one career requires. Now imagine every single human in the world having only the skills that are required for that one career. Blew your mind didn't it? He intentionally created us differently because He knew we would all be fulfilling different missions. We can't be praying to look like other people and praying to live like other families at the same time we are attempting to fulfill God's calling for our best life with our own families. It just doesn't work that way. Love who you are already and fall even more in love with who God has in mind for you to become. When we are attempting to be like someone else, we are basically complaining about who we already are. I'm all for living healthy and doing whatever is best for the temple God has given us, but don't pick something you want to look like based on what someone else looks like. At this point you have created a happiness scale and have placed your happiness point in something that is possible won't be filled. I can assure you that the world won't love you more at a size zero than they do at a size twenty. I can also assure you that if perhaps for some reason someone does, then they have a lot of personal issues of their own that they need to work out with God. Leave that up to Him and fall more in love with you.

Thinking positively about ourselves is a must for a positive lifestyle. Thinking positively is the key to a faith filled life. As I shared with you in a previous chapter, negative thinking use to be a natural trait I housed for many years and though most may not have realized how often I thought negatively, the bottom line is, I did. Just because someone may not necessarily portray they are a negative thinker because they don't voice it, doesn't mean that they aren't. I once was one of those people and the first thing I had to change in regards to that were my thoughts. I had to become more aware of my thoughts. This led me to realize how much my thoughts affected how I felt. Thankfully, we do have the capability to change ourselves but we have to be prepared to put in a lot of effort and we have to be disciplined to not waiver in the moments we want to go back to our comfort zone, our old ways. It's possible though because I've done it and it's worth it too so decide today to make it a point to be more intentional in positive thinking. It will then lead you to having more self awareness and it will give you the opportunity to be more in control of the only thing you have control over, you. You have to if you want to change the world.

Anytime we complain it automatically opens a window for negativity. We don't even have to voice the complaint for it to become something. We can simply think of a complaint and it puts our mind into a negative state rather we realize it or not. After a lot of praying for God to change my heart and to change me into a becoming a better example of Jesus, these negative thoughts started being easier for me to recognize and immediately change them to something positive. I would change something that originally started as a complaint to a sweet little gratitude prayer. I have a perfect example for you and if you have children you can totally relate. After we work all day, we have to come home to what is basically like a second job for most of us. We are tired. We have cooked, we have cleaned up the kitchen, and everyone is bathed and snuggled up in their beds and right as I snuggle in and get comfy under my covers, from the bedroom of the princess I hear, "Mommy, I want some milk." It's easy to go in to "Oh my goodness you have got to be kidding me. I just laid down." I'm not going to pretend that sometimes I don't say that or think that. One simple statement to cancel that whole negative thought or comment is, "Thank you Lord for that baby." It's not always easy to nip a negative thought in the bud and not let that thought then lead to a negative feeling that could potentially lead to so many other negative things, but I can assure you that it's worth it.

I'm pretty careful about where I allow my energy to go and I would advise you to be as well. I'm not a fan at all for giving other things permission to bring me down and essentially that's exactly what we do when we allow someone or a situation to get to us. The world will take the life out of us if we let it. Anytime I find myself feeling anything less than joyful or at peace, that means I've given something else the power to be able to do that. Don't give anything other than yourself the power to do that. Make it a point to not allow this to happen in order to maintain your most peaceful state. If perhaps you do find yourself at this point, immediately start figuring out how to get back to your state of peace rather its putting up a boundary toward a person, a situation, or even your own thought.

Simply put, life is simple. I'm sure you are wondering exactly what type of life I'm living in to be in a chaotic world like this thinking there is a way to make it simple. Honestly, I used to wonder the same thing myself, but the reality is that life is in fact simple, we just make it difficult. If you want a peaceful life without chaos and madness, make one. You have the power to change that rather you believe it or not.

You, my dear friend, stay humble. Stop sweating the small things. Forgive people. The only thing worth fighting for is love. Make what someone else thinks of you, the least of your concern. Don't make choices for your life based on someone else's opinion. Don't live life in fear. If you feel as if you have been called to do something, stop waiting and go do it. Don't ever miss an opportunity to share God with someone rather they believe in Him or not. If you know they don't believe, love them more. Know that we can change from old ways and not be defined by who we may have been in the past. Everything happens for a reason and things work for the greatest good of those who love God. Change your mind and fixate your eyes on God so that He can change your heart. Don't ever stop sharing His love and the amazing things He has done in your life. When we get to heaven, there is only one thing from this earth that will go with us and those are people. Bring as many people as you can to heaven with you and don't forget that the only way to do that is through love.